Presented to

_____

By

_____

On the Occasion of

_____

Date

_____

INSPIRING WORDS
FOR WOMEN

Thoughts of Hope and Encouragement
When You Need Them

Darlene Sala

BARBOUR
PUBLISHING

Cover design by Charles Brock, The DesignWorks Group, Inc.
www.thedesignworksgroup.com

Published by Barbour Publishing, Inc., P.O. Box 719, Uhrichsville, Ohio 44683
www.barbourbooks.com

Our mission is to publish and distribute inspirational products offering exceptional value and biblical encouragement to the masses.

ecpa Member of the
Evangelical Christian
Publishers Association

Printed in China.
5 4 3 2 1

DEDICATION

To my husband,
Harold—
Thank you for your encouragement
and inspiration
and your understanding during those times
when I "tuned out"
in order to write.
You are part of every page—
and the joy of my life.

CONTENTS

WHEN YOU WANT TO GROW—
Inspiration to Be More Like Christ

WHEN TOUGH TIMES COME—
Inspiration for Days When You Feel Like Quitting

WHEN YOU WANT TO KNOW GOD BETTER—
Inspiration to Have a Closer Relationship

WHEN YOU WANT TO MAKE A DIFFERENCE—
Inspiration to Influence the Lives of Others

INTRODUCTION

"Look at that orchid! See the delicate markings and shading? Absolutely gorgeous! Just *look* at it!"

Yes, when I see a beautiful flower, I immediately want to tell someone else about it. I want to grab your arm and pull you over to share its loveliness, the exquisite color, the unusual formation of the petals. Terri, my walking partner, is getting used to my exclamations as we pass by exquisite flowers. She knows I just *have* to exclaim about them.

I'm the same way about majestic mountains, or multihued tropical fish, or brand-new babies. Beauty is just plain meant to be shared. Enjoying beauty takes us out of the doldrums of our despondency and lifts our eyes and our hearts from the muck we're slogging through to the loveliness of God's handiwork.

For that same reason I love to share thoughts from God's Word that have helped or challenged me. Sometimes they're expressions of God's love. Or sometimes there's a promise that He will help us when we're at the end of our rope. Other times we find encouragement when we already know what God wants us to do but we just need the motivation to get going.

That's what *Inspiring Words for Women* is about—just sharing the beauty of God's Word.

I like the title the publishers have chosen. "To inspire" comes from Latin roots meaning "to breathe." The Bible is God-breathed—inspired by God Himself (see 2 Timothy 3:16), and that is why it carries such weight in our lives. Job says, "It is the spirit in a man, the breath of the Almighty [the word is "inspiration" in the *King James Version*], that gives him understanding."

Of course, this book is not "inspired" in that sense. But I do pray that the scriptures contained in the selections will inspire you in your Christian life and motivate you to obey God's still, small voice as He speaks to you from His Word. If you are moved to not give up during the hard times but follow the Lord more closely, the book will have achieved its purpose.

Once again my thanks go to Ellyn Sanna for her editing work. I've never known an editor who could "get into an author's head and heart" so well. She is a joy!

Need inspiration for today? Come, take a look.

WHEN YOU HAVE A BIG NEED

Inspiration for

Believing God Will Provide

Is Anything
Too Hard for God?

One night God gave Abraham an astronomy lesson. He told him to go outdoors and "Look up at the heavens and count the stars—if indeed you can count them"—which, of course, he couldn't. Then God made an incredible promise to Abraham: "So shall your offspring be" (Genesis 15:5). As many descendants as the stars in the sky? Yes, that's what God promised.

There was only one little problem. Abraham had no children at all! On top of that, he was already old—*really* old, and so was his wife, Sarah. What a pledge! God had just promised elderly, childless Abraham offspring as countless as the stars!

Yet the Bible says, "Abram believed the LORD, and he credited it to him as righteousness" (Genesis 15:6). And sure enough, when Abraham was 100 and Sarah was 90, baby Isaac was born, the beginning of the Jewish people, who now are more than can be counted. That's truly amazing!

Abraham faced an insurmountable problem. Is the situation you are facing any more difficult than that? In fact, that's almost exactly what God asked Abraham in Genesis 18:14: "Is anything too hard for the LORD? I will return to you at the appointed time next year and Sarah will have a son."

Be assured that God will keep His promises to you every bit as much as to Abraham because His nature never changes. The word "impossible" is not in God's vocabulary. Note these verses:

1. **Mark 10:27:** Jesus said, "With man this is impossible, but not with God; all things are possible with God."

2. **Luke 18:27:** Jesus replied, "What is impossible with men is possible with God."

3. **Luke 1:37:** "For nothing is impossible with God."

What situation are you facing today? Go outside and look up at the stars. Are your circumstances bigger than the God who made those stars and assigned them their places in the universe?

"Have faith in God," said Jesus in Mark 11:22. Not faith in your faith, or in an easy solution, or in yourself, or in money, or in any human help, or even in your own insight to understand the problem. But have faith in the One who is far greater, wiser, and richer, and who has the perspective of eternity—GOD.

TAKE A BREATH

The next time your circumstances seem too big to handle, make a list of all the things that are overwhelming you. Putting your troubles in writing often helps to define them; it gives them boundaries instead of allowing them to fill your thoughts in a vague, confusing cloud. Once you have your list, go through it item by item and imagine yourself placing each circumstance or worry in God's hands. Do this as often as you need to throughout the day—and remind yourself that those hands are the same ones that created the universe.

*Loving God, thank You that You're as creative
at solving my problems as You are at making stars.*

But You Promised. . .

A young woman calls on the phone in tears. "I pray and pray and pray about this problem, but prayer just doesn't work! This has gone on for eight years now. Nothing changes. I can't take it any longer! I've had it with God!"

Another friend, recently widowed, also struggles with trusting God. "Three times God gave me assurance that my husband would be healed. Each time it was from the chapter I was reading in my quiet time. Yet my husband died. How can I find guidance from the Bible in the future? How can I trust God's promises?"

Well, what about those promises? Jesus said, "If two of you on earth agree about anything you ask for, it will be done for you by my Father in heaven" (Matthew 18:19). He also said, "Ask and it will be given to you; seek and you will find; knock and the door will be opened to you" (Matthew 7:7).

But what if instead of the door opening, it is slammed in your face? What if you ask and ask and ask, and nothing changes?

We had promised our kids a certain outing—and then, unavoidably, had to change our plans. "But you *promised*," they reminded us with disappointment and disbelief written all over their faces. You may have said the same thing to God.

I don't have all the answers. But I do read that Jesus said, "Do not let your hearts be troubled. Trust in God" (John 14:1), and it's that word "trust" that stands out to me. Oh, yes, trust is easy when you can see what God is doing and why He is doing it. "When the Israelites saw the great power the LORD displayed against the Egyptians, the people. . . put their trust in him" (Exodus 14:31). That kind of trust is easy when God answers yes to your prayer. Or when, like the song in *Oklahoma*, you can sing, "Oh, what a beautiful morning. . .everything's going my way."

But trusting when you *can't* see why your prayer isn't answered the way you asked—well, that's another matter. Yet, as hard as it seems, when you get right down to it, that's what trusting is all about. The only thing to do when God doesn't answer the way you thought He would, is to "Trust in the LORD with all your heart and lean not on your own understanding" (Proverbs 3:5).

If you hold on to Him, "the God of hope [will] fill you with all joy and peace as you trust in him, so that you may overflow with hope by the power of the Holy Spirit" (Romans 15:13). It's the hope that eventually will fill your heart when you trust Him in the middle of your disappointment.

TAKE A BREATH

Keeping a prayer journal is a wonderful way to remind yourself of God's faithfulness. Some prayers may be answered while you're still shaping the thought in you mind; others may take years to be answered. Sometimes, you may plainly see God's pattern unfolding in your life; other times, His actions may seem puzzling or even disappointing. But if you make a regular habit of jotting down your prayers and God's answers, you'll be able to look back at your own personal testimony of God's trustworthiness. When your faith is wobbly, you can lean on those past experiences of God's love and care.

God, sometimes I don't understand why You allow
events to unfold the way they do. When that happens,
and I'm stumbling in the dark, help me to cling
even tighter to Your hand.

God Knows
Where the Fish Are

Do you have a financial need right now? Oh, not the kind where you say, "I need some money to go shopping at that sale in the mall." A *real* need.

Some of Jesus' disciples did. So they went fishing—all night on the Sea of Galilee. John tells about it in chapter 21 of his gospel. Early in the morning, Jesus called to them from the shore, "Friends, haven't you any fish?"

"No," they answered.

He said, "Throw your net on the right side of the boat and you will find some." When they did, they were unable to haul the net in because of the large number of fish.

Jesus knew exactly where those fish were!

Another time, Peter reminded Jesus that the taxes were due—the temple tax. Jesus told him to go to the lake and throw out a line. "Take the first fish you catch; open its mouth and you will find a four-drachma coin. Take it and give it to them for my tax and yours" (Matthew 17:27).

Clearly, Jesus knew how to supply the answer to each need. And God knows how to meet your need, too. He knows where to find the "fish" in your life.

I often think that God must smile as He watches people on earth digging for gold or precious jewels. All the time they're working and sweating, He knows how much yet-undiscovered treasure lies hidden all around them. Now, if they would dig a little farther to the north. . .

If God knows where the fish are—and where the gold is—surely He can meet your need as well. Perhaps the reason He has not yet answered is that He wants you to seek *Him,* not just the money. If you have a child who cares only about your money and what you can give him, and he never gives you a hug or tells you he loves you or wants to be around you, you get pretty tired of just forking over the cash. In a similar way, God also wants our affection and love.

In Matthew 6:33, Jesus gave us the basis for having our needs met when He said: "But seek first his kingdom and his righteousness, and all these things will be given to you as well." Clearly, God's supply is based on our relationship with Him. When you are His child, He finds joy in giving to you, for He said, "If you. . .know how to give good gifts to your children, how much more will your Father in heaven give good gifts to those who ask him!" (Matthew 7:11).

Your need is no surprise to your Father. Seek Him instead of His gifts, and in His time, He'll show you where the "fish" are. He will meet that need.

TAKE A BREATH

Be sure God knows it's not just the money you're after. When you pray, make a habit of telling God how much you love Him *before* you start on your list of needs. This practice isn't only for God's benefit; it will remind your own heart what is truly most important. When you are in a close love relationship with God, you'll find you can more easily trust Him while you wait for His answers.

Father, You know the longings of my heart.
Thank You that I can depend on You to meet my every need.

How Long Is God's Arm?

When you have a big need, God can seem far, far away. That's because your need is very close to you—looming large on the horizon and blocking your vision of everything else, including God. As you look up to the Lord, all you can see is your huge need filling your entire range of vision. When that happens, it's time to step back and get a new perspective.

Over and over and over in the Old Testament we read God's words that "by his mighty hand and outstretched arm" He did something for His people or will do something for them in the future. Whether it was to free them from slavery or redeem them from some foreign oppressor, God said He would reach out with His outstretched arm and act on their behalf.

That leads us to ask, "How long is God's arm, anyway?"

Actually, I don't know the answer to that question. But I can assure you that it is long enough! Yes, God's arm is long enough and strong enough to reach down and meet the need in your life that right now seems so enormous to you.

"Surely the arm of the LORD is not too short to save,"

said Isaiah (59:1). Now, in case you don't think Isaiah knew what he was talking about, remember that he was the prophet who saw the Lord with his own eyes (see Isaiah 6). If Isaiah says the Lord's arm is long enough—and he was an eyewitness—then we can trust his testimony.

Job, you remember, was the man whose patience was tried with many overwhelming difficulties. His friend Elihu sought to give him advice in all his problems, so he told Job that God is beyond our understanding (Job 36:26) and that He is beyond our reach (Job 37:23). Well, from a human standpoint that is true. We cannot reach up to heaven to bring God down to us. But even though our arms aren't long enough to reach God, His mighty outstretched arm is plenty long to reach down to us and to meet us at our point of deepest need.

If you ever wonder if God's arm is long enough to meet your need, remember that it was by that same great arm that God created the heavens and the earth. "Ah, Sovereign LORD, you have made the heavens and the earth by your great power and outstretched arm," said Jeremiah (32:17).

And then Jeremiah added those heartening words: "Nothing is too hard for you"! That includes *your* need. Absolutely nothing is too hard for the God whose mighty hand and outstretched arm reaches right down to where you live.

TAKE A BREATH

Do you ever find yourself limiting God's power? Sure, you know God did amazing things in times past—but you can't find the faith to believe He can reach down into the circumstances of your own life. We all feel like that sometimes—but remember, that's all it is: a feeling. Our human thoughts and emotions will never shorten God's arm.

So the next time you feel yourself doubting God's power in your life, remind yourself that your feelings are transitory; they'll come and go—but God's mighty strength never changes.

Mighty God, thank You for loving me enough
to reach out to me, no matter how far away I feel.

WHEN FRIENDS GET RICH
AND YOU DON'T

A young woman called me on the telephone utterly discouraged. "My husband works hard, and so do I," she explained. "But we never seem to get ahead financially. We give to the Lord's work and are involved in serving the Lord. Yet we're always a little short. This has gone on for years now, and it's hard on my husband's self-esteem and mine, too. I look at my friends and see them climbing the financial ladder. They're remodeling their homes and sending their kids to the best schools. I used to go shopping with these friends, but now we don't even shop at the same stores anymore." I could hear the despair in her voice.

"My husband and I pray and pray about our financial needs," she continued, "but nothing happens. God *could* meet our need—so why doesn't He? He is the God who raises the dead. That means He has all power; He could change any circumstance we face—if He wanted to."

I didn't have a quick answer for her. I just wanted to hold this young woman in my arms for a while because I knew she was hurting. We began to talk about her options.

When we don't like it that God is not meeting needs in our lives, clearly we have two choices:

1. To turn away from God and become bitter, or

2. to turn to God and continue to rely totally on Him even though we don't understand what He is doing.

It's pretty obvious that Option #1 is not a good choice. Hebrews 12:15 warns us to "watch out that no bitterness takes root among you, for as it springs up it causes deep trouble, hurting many" (TLB). No, turning from God is not a good choice.

That leaves us Option #2: turning to God and continuing to rely on Him. When you choose to wait on God, you give up relying on any logical reason you can figure out for what is happening. You simply say, "God, I make a choice to depend on You and no one else. I throw myself on You. I will continue to ask You to solve this problem I face, but if You don't meet my need the way I think You should, I will trust You anyway. You must have a reason I can't see."

Like the three Hebrews who were thrown into the fiery furnace, you say, "If we are thrown into the blazing furnace, the God we serve is able to save us from it. . .but even if he does not," we will not turn our backs on Him (Daniel 3:17–18). (By the way, if you think they burned up, read the rest of the story.)

Let's say you decide God has let you down and you just can't trust Him for what you need. Whom will you trust?

When some of the crowds turned back and no longer followed Jesus, He asked the twelve disciples if they wanted to leave, too. Peter, who had his times when he didn't rely on the Lord, was the first one this time who spoke up: "Lord, to whom would we go? You alone have the words that give eternal life" (John 6:68 NLT).

What happened to my friend who called on the phone? Just when she was at a point of despair, God supplied her need through a source she had long given up on. Oh, she is not "rich," but her needs have been met and her faith has grown. She knows that God keeps His promise.

Dear friend, don't give up. Paul assured us, "And this same God who takes care of me will supply all your needs from his glorious riches, which have been given to us in Christ Jesus" (Philippians 4:19 NLT). He didn't say "when," but he did say God would do it. Perhaps you won't be as rich as your friends are, but He has promised His supply for your need. "Be joyful in hope, patient in affliction, faithful in prayer" (Romans 12:12) until the answer comes.

TAKE A BREATH

When you feel as though you're at the end of your rope—whether emotionally, financially, or physically—it often helps to talk things over with a trusted friend who can offer a spiritual perspective on your situation. She probably won't have a "magic" answer—but just sharing our burdens usually makes them feel lighter. That's one reason why the apostle Paul referred to the church as the body of Christ—so we can work together to carry the heavy loads of life.

Dear God, help me to be "joyful in hope,"
even when the circumstances of my life are most discouraging.
Remind me that You have promised to share with me
Your glorious riches.

Praying until
Faith Comes

"Whatever you ask for in prayer," said Jesus, "believe that you have received it, and it will be yours" (Mark 11:24). That's a wonderful promise, especially when you have a big need! Somehow, though, telling me I must believe in order to receive sometimes discourages me. I realize how weak my faith is.

My dad, who was a preacher for more than seventy years, came to grips with this issue in the early years of his ministry. Here's what he said:

> Let me encourage you, if you're facing a great test, if there is a very desperate need in your life, don't try to work up faith in your heart. Get alone with God. Read His Word, look up into the face of God and ask Him to give you His faith. When the faith of God is imparted to your heart, then nothing is impossible.

He learned this lesson through personal experience

when I was about eighteen months old. I had developed a cold that went into ear infections. At that time, little could be done for earaches except to keep the ears warm—and pray. But instead of improving, I got worse. The pediatrician warned them that if the ears stuck out straight with no crease behind, this would be a sign of mastoid, a serious condition that might require chiseling through the bone at the back of the ear in order to relieve the pressure—not a pleasant thought to any parent!

The next day the worst-case scenario occurred: both ears were at right angles to my head. My dad went to the church to pray. He had been preaching to others that God could heal our bodies, and now his faith was put to the test.

After a period of intense prayer, all of a sudden, it seemed to him that a great big chunk of faith dropped right down into his heart. He looked up and said, "Lord, we're going to trust you."

That evening he and my mom began praying again by my crib. I would toss and cry, and then fall into an exhausted sleep, only to wake and cry again. They prayed on through the evening, hour after hour, holding on to God.

My dad said later:

I remember telling the Lord, "Your Word says, 'I am the LORD, who heals you' (Exodus 15:26). Lord, I don't know what it means except what it says. Some may think it means one thing and some may think it means another, but, Lord, all I know is what it says: 'I am the LORD who heals you,' and I'm going to take it for what it says."

About one o'clock in the morning, a clear sense of confidence came into his heart: "Suddenly I knew! I didn't open my eyes; I didn't look at my baby; I knew in my heart that something had happened. 'My baby's healed,' I said, 'My baby's healed!'"

At 7:30 that morning, my parents awoke to my singing and cooing in the crib. When they got up to take a look, they saw that both ears were perfectly flat to my head, and the substance that had poured out of my ears was on the pillow cover. For years my mom kept the pillowcase as a remembrance of what God did that night.

Have you been trying to "work up" some faith? The Bible says, "Faith comes by hearing, and hearing by the word of God" (Romans 10:17 NKJV). Stand firm on God's promises, and then seek His face until He implants faith in your heart. He has heard and will answer your need—but His power and action do not depend on your efforts.

TAKE A BREATH

When your faith is at its lowest, that's the time to read the Bible. Turn your attention away from your doubts, away from your situation, away from all that is causing you so much distress. Instead, look at God as He reveals Himself to you through the scripture.

Remember when Peter tried to walk on the water? He did just fine until he stopped looking at Jesus—and then he started to sink. It's the same principle we're talking about here. As the author of Hebrews wrote (12:2), when we fix our eyes on Jesus, He is the author and finisher of our faith.

Lord, the water all around me seems awfully cold and deep— but I'm keeping my eyes on You. Don't let me sink.

WHEN YOU STRUGGLE WITH YOUR PAST

Inspiration for Days
When Memories Burn

I Can't Remember!

One of my friend's early recollections happened at a party. Her grandmother had been chatting for some time with another woman who was a relative by marriage. Suddenly she came up short and remarked to my friend, "I shouldn't be talking to her. I'm mad at her!"

"Why, what did she do to you?" asked my friend.

There was a long pause. Finally her grandmother replied, "I can't remember!"

Warren Walker says that three things drag us down in life: a burden on the back, sin in the heart, or a chip on the shoulder.[1] How true! Yet, like that grandmother, many of us hold on to the heavy weight of a chip on the shoulder.

A chip on the shoulder is a hurt that has never healed. It is a tight band around the heart that constricts the flow of love. It is a caustic acid that eats into a friendship until little is left of a relationship that once brought joy.

Why do we hold on to hurts? Maybe because we actually enjoy mulling over how right we were and how wrong the other person was. Perhaps we self-righteously reason that the person who offended us has never asked for forgiveness, so we aren't obligated to forgive until she does.

Usually we hold on to hurts as a matter of pride. Neither party wants to make the first move to settle the matter. "Why should I go to her? It was *her* fault! If I approach her first, it means I'm admitting I was wrong—and I wasn't!"

Scripture is very plain, however, about who should make the first move. "If another believer sins against you, go privately and point out the fault" (Matthew 18:15 NLT).

What do you have to lose? Absolutely nothing—except a few bruises to your ego, perhaps. And what is there to gain? A lot!

First, you may just possibly regain a relationship with this person. Jesus said, "If the other person listens and confesses it, you have won that person back."

Second, you will have that good feeling inside that you have done what God wants you to do. You have obeyed His instruction.

Third, you will be an example to those who are watching you. Others just might find the courage to settle their differences because you did.

"Make every effort to live in peace with all men," said the writer of Hebrews. Then he continued, "See to it that. . . no bitter root grows up to cause trouble and defile many" (Hebrews 12:14–15).

Whether it's a chip on your shoulder that irritates your peace of mind or a root of bitterness that taints your attitude, settle it once and for all. If you do, never again will you feel that irritating prod of conscience that reminds you of unfinished business.

Author's Note: Just today I had to "practice what I preach." Phew, I'm glad that's done! That chip on the shoulder was getting pretty heavy.

TAKE A BREATH

Take an honest look at your heart. Make note of any lack of forgiveness you may be harboring. Now take positive action to rebuild the relationship. Don't put it off. At least put the ball in the other person's court. He or she can choose to forgive you or not—either way, you need to be free of the load of anger you've been carrying.

Dear Gardener of my soul—
dig out any roots of bitterness growing in my heart.

WRONG CHOICES

She had made wrong choices. And now she lived with the consequences. Too ashamed to come to the well to fill her water pot in the morning as other women did, she came at noon. As she approached, she saw a man sitting on the well, resting.

"Will you give me a drink?" the man asked her.

She, who was rarely shocked by anything, was taken aback. "You are a Jew and I am a Samaritan woman. How can you ask me for a drink?"

After all, Jews didn't associate with Samaritans.

"If you knew the gift of God and who it is that asks you for a drink," the man replied, "you would have asked him and he would have given you living water. . . . Everyone who drinks this water will be thirsty again, but. . .the water I give him will become in him a spring of water welling up to eternal life."

Not understanding what He was offering her, she replied, "Sir, give me this water so that I won't get thirsty and have to keep coming here to draw water."

At that the man said, "Go, call your husband and come back." When the woman replied that she had no husband, the man responded, "You are right. . . . The fact is, you have had five husbands, and the man you now have is not your husband."

Immediately, this woman, whose life was so cut off from social acceptance because of her wrong choices, sensed that she was not speaking to any ordinary person. Before the day was over, she realized she had met Jesus the Messiah, the very Son of God (John 4). He reached out to her with forgiveness and eternal life.

When you think of God, do you sense that your wrong choices have erected a wall between you and Him—perhaps a wall of fear or shame? It doesn't have to be that way. The Bible says, "But now in Christ Jesus you who once were far away have been brought near through the blood of Christ. For he himself is our peace, who has made the two one and has destroyed the barrier, the dividing wall of hostility. . . through the cross" (Ephesians 2:13–16).

Perhaps you're struggling with accepting God's forgiveness for your sins. Maybe you're thinking, "If you knew how bad my sin is—and that it was totally my own fault—you'd understand I don't deserve forgiveness."

Take heart. That day at the well in Samaria, Jesus crossed major boundaries—racial, cultural, social, and religious—to reach out to a woman who needed forgiveness. In fact, He *purposely* passed through her town to bring salvation to her needy, thirsty heart.

Know that Jesus still crosses every boundary to reach out to you. No sin is too bad to be forgiven. He died for every sin you have ever committed. The Savior knows your past—yet He offers full forgiveness.

Come to Him and simply admit your need—then accept His offer of pardon for every sin you have ever committed. He will give you the water of life that truly satisfies.

TAKE A BREATH

What walls have you built between you and Jesus? Jesus has already spanned each of these barriers with His cross. The walls exist only in your own mind.

Try making a list of each barrier you sense between you and God. Your list may be long—or it may have only one item, but that one thing may loom large and dark in your mind. Once you have your list, take it in prayer to Jesus. You may want to prayerfully burn each item to symbolize the reality of Christ's forgiveness. Or you might want to discuss the "walls" with a trusted friend or spiritual leader; sometimes we can finally grasp God's forgiveness when it's spoken to us with a human voice. Whatever action you choose to take, do not let any wall remain in your mind. Bring each barrier in prayer to Jesus until you can finally see the reality of His forgiveness.

When I was all alone, trapped within the walls of my sin,
You reached out Your hand to me. Thank You, Jesus.

LIVING BEYOND THE
CONSEQUENCES

Sometimes women tell me they know God has forgiven their sins, but they can't forgive themselves. Often the sin they are struggling with is related to some area of sexuality.

Perhaps you struggle with this. When it comes to sex, like the Samaritan woman in John 4, somewhere you made wrong choices, and you are deeply sorry. Or maybe you were a victim of sexual abuse or assault. In either case, you may find it very hard to break off that sexual relationship; even if you have broken it off, you may not be able to stop thinking about it. Although it may be in the past and you are now happily married, that memory can creep into your consciousness at the most ill-timed moments. (Perhaps your husband touches you a certain way, reminding you of the skeleton in the closet of your memory.) Whether it is premarital sex, extramarital sex, abortion, or sexual abuse, you feel that even if God has forgiven you, you deserve to suffer long-term. Deep in your heart, you feel sexual sin is different from other sins.

Actually, when it comes to consequences, you're partially right about that last part. The Bible tells us that sexual sin *is* different from other sins: "Run away from sexual sin! No other sin so clearly affects the body as this one does. For sexual immorality is a sin against your own body" (1 Corinthians 6:18 NLT).

Because of the way God made us, when a woman has sexual relations with a man, a God-planned bond is formed that is not only physical but emotional and perhaps spiritual as well. Authors Linda Dillow and Lorraine Pintus speak of this bond as "soul ties."[2] Of course, God's plan was for this bonding to take place in marriage—a tie that unites couples together when pressures outside their relationship would tear them apart.

But the end result is that when women have sex outside marriage, they often suffer long-term consequences. Like it or not, they have a bond with the one with whom they had a sexual encounter—whether the association was voluntary or involuntary—and that bond is not easily broken.

But be clear on this: The difference between sexual sins and other sins is not that God is reluctant to forgive sins related to sex. On the contrary, He died for *all* your sins, including sexual sins. But freedom from the sexual sin that haunts you comes only when you fully allow Jesus Christ to be Lord of every aspect of your life—your body, your emotions, and certainly your thoughts and memories.

Be encouraged, there is life beyond the consequences of

sexual sin—a glorious life of acceptance and healing. I like what Ruth Harms Calkin wrote:

> Nothing is too hard for You
> Not even me.[3]

TAKE A BREATH

If sexual sin weighs you down, say to God:

- From this point on I accept the truth that Jesus died for *all my sins* and that God has forgiven me completely, erasing my sins and failure.

- I embrace the fact that God looks upon me as a whole, cleansed, and forgiven woman.

- I, therefore, commit my life fully to Jesus Christ and to purity.

Once you have made this commitment, fill your mind with scripture—verses like Psalm 139:23–24; Ephesians 5:3; Philippians 4:8; 2 Timothy 2:22; and Hebrews 12:11. When you have misgivings, don't "stuff" them, but immediately talk to the Lord about your doubts. Find a trusted friend who will pray with you and hold you accountable when temptations come.

Jesus, thank You that Your forgiveness has made me whole.

A Pure Virgin

The bride in all her dazzling white glory stands at the back of the church waiting to walk down the aisle to be united with her handsome groom. Her eyes sparkle with anticipation. Ahead of her lie all the joys and intimacy of married life. It's a day most girls dream of from childhood.

God uses this beautiful image to help us understand the relationship He wants with us. One of the most beautiful word pictures in the Bible is the one where Jesus is pictured as the Bridegroom and believers as His bride: "Let us be glad and rejoice and honor him. For the time has come for the wedding feast of the Lamb, and his bride has prepared herself" (Revelation 19:7 NLT).

But this is an age when many brides have not kept themselves as virgins for their wedding day. Can God restore virginity?

In his book *The Mary Miracle*, Jack Hayford points out that in the ancient Roman world the word "Corinthian" became the common adjective for being "rotten to the core." The city of Corinth, located in what is present-day Greece, was known for its sin. In Paul's first letter to the Christians of Corinth, he lists some pretty sinful characters, including those who struggled with sexual sins—adulterers, sexually immoral, prostitutes, and homosexual offenders. He personalizes it when he adds, "And that is what some of you were."

The good news is that Paul goes on to declare, "But you were washed, you were sanctified, you were justified in the name of the Lord Jesus" (1 Corinthians 6:11). It would be wonderful enough to be washed, sanctified, and clean. But in his second letter to the Corinthians, Paul adds an even more astounding thought when he writes, "I promised you to one husband, to Christ, so that I might present you as a pure virgin to him" (2 Corinthians 11:2).

Hayford says:

Do you hear that, dear one? *A chaste virgin.* Look at this awesome new creation statement in God's Word! See how former sin and sex addicts are now being declared "virginal"! Can you imagine a more towering statement on how vast the possibilities of God's restorative powers are, once He sets about recovering ruined, broken or sin-stained people?[4]

That means that if you have accepted Christ's death on the cross as payment for your sins and have placed your faith in Him as your Savior, God looks on you as a pure virgin—with a heart just as white and clean as the glories of a radiant bride.

If you struggle with believing God truly wipes out your

sexual sins, remember that "if we confess our sins to him, he is faithful and just to forgive us and to cleanse us from every wrong" (1 John 1:9 NLT).

A pure virgin! A new start! Live in that truth.

TAKE A BREATH

When a memory of what you've done in the past pops into your mind, say to yourself out loud, "Jesus died for that sin of _____," and then name it. Then say, "I have confessed it to Him, and according to His Word, He has forgiven me," and put it out of your mind. Remember that He promises to cleanse us from *all* sin—not from all but sexual sins, but *all* wrong we've ever done.

Because of You, dear Lord, I am pure from head to toe, on the inside and the outside. Thank You for this wonderful gift. Help me to stop looking over my shoulder at the past and instead walk forward, clothed in Your purity.

FERTILIZER ON MY ROSES

In her writings "Lessons from a Rose," my friend Julie Garvey speaks about a facet of growing roses that we don't usually care to focus on—fertilizing. Yet fertilizer is a very necessary part of growing beautiful blooms. Julie says that from her experience, the best fertilizer to produce lovely roses is, unfortunately, the natural type that smells atrocious. No one likes the odor, but everyone likes the results. This fertilizer she compares to the painful experiences of life, especially those that come through the difficult people we all bump into in life.

"When I look at or 'smell' the events by themselves, they smell horrible and seem so unnecessary," writes Julie. "Yet when I look at the purpose of compost, I know that God has used this, too, in my life to add richness to the soil of my heart so that as I grow, my roots are strong and the bush is sturdy."[5]

Yes, fertilizer stinks! Perhaps in your life, it was an unkind act by a member of your family. Or possibly you had your hopes for the future dashed by cruel circumstances. Whatever the painful experience, be encouraged—you will be richer for what you have endured—if you allow God to cultivate this experience into the roots of your life.

Alexander Solzhenitsyn spent ten years in a Soviet work camp. In the midst of that hardship, he determined to transform his sufferings into some useful purpose. Later he would say, "I nourished my soul there, and I say without hesitation: 'Bless you, prison, for having been in my life.'"[6]

Isaiah too faced difficulty, but he eventually saw a purpose in what he endured: "Surely it was for my benefit that I suffered such anguish" (38:17). The writer of Hebrews said, "No discipline seems pleasant at the time, but painful. Later on, however, it produces a harvest of righteousness and peace for those who have been trained by it" (12:11).

Julie adds, "It is interesting to note that you do not add fertilizer to a rose until it begins to leaf out. It seems that has been the timing of many of these [painful] events in my life. Just when I was beginning to grow, I got another pile dumped on me. The gentle Gardener tills the soil with special relationships, His word, and music to help me absorb the proper nutrients. The tears that fall from my eyes water the fertilizer so that it doesn't burn the roots or just sit on top of the dirt. The roots must go deep, and this is one way that happens."[7]

In your life have you had a load of "fertilizer" dumped on you? Don't waste it. Think of it as something that God can use to cause the roses in your life to bloom—bigger and more fragrant than ever.

TAKE A BREATH

Make a list in your prayer journal of the "fertilizers" in your life right now. Now be patient while you wait for the "roses." As each one appears, be sure to jot it down in your journal next to the "compost" that lead to that particular bloom. As you move forward in life, you will have a wonderful reminder that God can bring beauty out of ugliness.

When my life seems full of compost,
give me patience, Lord, to wait for the roses.

What God Does
with Imperfections

I was born with a thumb-sized birthmark on my left cheek called a "port-wine stain." It was not an issue to me until I started school. "What's that on your face?" the other kids would ask, looking at me as if I were some kind of freak—or at least, that's how I felt.

My parents consulted a plastic surgeon about having it removed, but they were told that the resulting scar would be more noticeable than the birthmark. A sympathetic kindergarten teacher told them about a heavy cosmetic that would cover the blemish, and it did help—except that the question changed to "Why do you wear so much powder on your face?" Hardly much of an improvement for a six-year old! Furthermore, when I went swimming, the makeup washed off. I became very sensitive about my appearance.

One night at a church prayer meeting I got to thinking about the verse that says, "You may ask me for anything in my name, and I will do it" (John 14:14). I earnestly asked the Lord to remove my birthmark. That night I went home with the great hope that when I washed off my makeup, it would be gone. But there was no change.

Eventually, when I was a middle-aged adult, God answered my prayer by means of medical science. After a number of laser treatments, the mark is so light that it is hardly visible.

In 1999, I wrote a little book called *Created for a Purpose*. In it I say that our bodies are the frames for the works of art God wants to create in our lives. I tell how I struggled with shyness, thinking that if I were only an extrovert instead of an introvert, I would be of more value to God. Finally I realized that God had made me like I am because He wanted someone exactly like me. If He had wanted an extrovert, He would have made me one. But what He wanted was for me to live for Him with the talents and abilities He has given me, not the ones I wish I had.

Philippians 3:12 became special to me: "I press on to take hold of that for which Christ Jesus took hold of me"— not someone else's purpose, but mine—custom-made and possible with the power of the Holy Spirit.

Then it hit me. The birthmark was not a mistake. If I had not struggled with issues of self-consciousness and being "different" from others, I probably never would have written *Created for a Purpose*. I never would have received letters from women in prison who read the book and caught a glimpse of what they can be because God has a purpose for them. Or the truck driver who was living with drugs and alcohol—and her co-driver/boyfriend—when she picked up a copy of the book at a truck stop, and God spoke to her heart. She left the guy at the next stop and went back home to begin a new life with God. Or how about the hospital executive who was contemplating suicide when she spotted the book in the gift shop on a shelf high above her head? The message reached her heart and saved her life.

Were you thinking God made a mistake when He made you? No, dear friend, you are not a mistake. You are a potential work of art if you will just give yourself to God to use as He sees fit.

TAKE A BREATH

When you feel like a failure, don't dwell on your feelings of unworthiness. Instead, praise God for His power to create beauty and meaning in your life.

Lord, I give myself to You. Please use all the mixed up pieces of my life to create something beautiful for Your kingdom.

WHEN YOU WANT TO WANT TO GROW

Inspiration to Be
More Like Christ

NUMBER-ONE PRIORITY

I admit it—I'm a confirmed list-maker. Right or wrong, I operate on the premise that if I make a list of everything I need to do, I'll get more done than if I just do the first thing that pops into my head.

Do I usually get everything crossed off the list? Rarely, but as someone wrote, "The Lord didn't do it all in one day. What makes me think I can?"

The number-one item on my to-do list every day is my personal time with God, made up primarily of Bible reading and prayer. But I've discovered that this time can become very routine:

1. Read a chapter of the Bible, and

2. Run through my prayer request list.

Done! "Devotions" checked off! I feel a sense of satisfaction because I've made God happy, and now I can get on with the next item on my list!

But is that really what it takes to make God happy? Where does the Bible say, "If you want to please Me, you shall read one chapter of the Bible every day. Then you shall recite to Me the list of everything you want."

What, then, are *God's* priorities? A very intelligent man, an expert in God's laws, once asked Jesus that question: "Which is the greatest commandment?" (Matthew 22:34–40). He was really saying, "What is the number-one priority, Jesus?"

Jesus replied, " 'Love the Lord your God with all your heart and with all your soul and with all your mind.' This is the first and greatest commandment. And the second is like it: 'Love your neighbor as yourself' "(Matthew 22:37–39).

If you're a stay-at-home mom, your to-do list may include such exciting jobs as making sure the laundry gets done, the groceries purchased, and the kids taken to their music lessons. If you're a career woman, your life isn't necessarily filled with exciting duties either. Checking inventory and filling out reports gets pretty repetitious even if you work in a beautiful office behind a mahogany desk.

Yet you can hallow all these jobs by loving God with all your heart while you do them. You can love your neighbor as yourself by being sensitive to his or her needs. As you go about your work, you can watch for opportunities to show genuine love to those you meet: that clerk whose eyes reveal heartache, the delivery man whose gruff response speaks volumes about his frustration with life, or the obnoxious neighbor who keeps your son's basketball when it goes over the wall into his yard.

Love God, and love others—it's really pretty simple. Yet it's what matters most to God. Putting those priorities into practice will permeate everything else I do all day long. I'll think about that today as I go through my to-do list.

TAKE A BREATH

Many businesses and organizations have a mission statement, an "umbrella" philosophy that gives direction to everything they do. Try making Matthew 22:37–39 your personal "mission statement." Write it on your date calendar, post it on your screen saver, tape it over your washing machine or on the visor of your car. Remind yourself often of the "umbrella" that arches over each of your to-do lists.

You know how forgetful I am, Lord—
so remind me over and over that love is
Your number-one priority for my life.

I Want My Own Way!

After speaking to a group of young adult singles in Macau, China, on giving their lives totally to Jesus Christ, I opened the session for questions and answers. A young girl stood and candidly asked, "I'm not a very obedient person. What should I do about this?"

I thought to myself, *You dear, honest girl! You have just summed up the human race! I'm not a very obedient person either, and neither is anyone else in this room!*

I want my own way! The prophet Isaiah said it like this: "We all, like sheep, have gone astray, each of us has turned to his own way" (Isaiah 53:6). It's probably the biggest struggle of my life—doing what God wants each moment instead of what I want.

It takes courage and faith to put your life in God's hands and obey Him implicitly. Madame Guyon calls it "abandonment." She says, "Abandonment is practiced by *continually* losing your own will in the will of God; by plunging your will into the depths of *His* will, there to be lost forever!"[8]

My will lost forever? It's scary to think of losing myself. When I get right down to it, "self" is actually my only possession. Notice, though, that God doesn't ask us to abandon ourselves into nothingness. He says, "My son [or daughter], give me your heart" (Proverbs 23:26). He's asking us to turn over to Him the foundation of our will—the heart.

And who would ever be more trustworthy with my heart than the God who, first, made me and second, sacrificed His Son that I might have a relationship with Him? The bottom line is that He has my best interests at heart. After all, He loves me! He, more than any other, will choose what is most excellent for me.

Obeying God sometimes feels like jumping off a high dive. "Here we go, Lord! Whee!" Just remember when you "abandon" yourself to Him, you jump right into the ocean of His love. He is there to catch you and hold you. And He will make sure you are safe in life's deep waters.

When you get right down to it, what more secure place could there be?

TAKE A BREATH

If you, like the young girl in Macau, are not a very "obedient person," try E. B. Pusey's advice: "When you wake, or as soon as you are dressed, offer up your whole self to God, soul and body, thoughts and purposes and desires, to be for that day what He wills."[9] Then hang on for an adventure!

You know, Lord, how often I seek guarantees, how I'd rather hedge my bets before I take a plunge. Give me a daring heart. Help me to leap into Your arms, knowing You will never let me fall.

What Has
Happened to Me. . . ?

The apostle Paul was in prison—not a clean, heated concrete cell, but a dank, stone hole-in-the-ground type of place. No doubt moisture trickled down the moldy, filth-encrusted walls, and the food was barely edible. Missing was any Glade air freshener to camouflage the odors. Yet from this discouraging spot, Paul wrote, "Now I want you to know, brothers, that what has happened to me has really served to advance the gospel" (Philippians 1:12).

Under those circumstances, how would most of us finish this statement: "What has happened to me has really served to. . ."?

Would we add, as Paul did, "advance the gospel"? Would we even care?

Perhaps we'd say, "It has certainly served to make me realize how good I had it up until now." Or, "It makes me wish I were out of here!" Most of us are more concerned about how the circumstances of life affect us personally than how they affect the kingdom of God.

How was the gospel advanced by Paul's being in chains in

such a miserable place? He tells us in Philippians 1:13–14:

1. The palace guard (and everyone else) knew he was there "for Christ."

2. Christians were encouraged to speak the Word more courageously and fearlessly.

Someone commented that it was not Paul who was chained to the guards; it was the guards who were chained to Paul! I'm sure every soldier who served a watch in that prison heard how to be born again. Yet as they watched his walk, they saw it measured up to his talk. Fellow believers, who must have been wondering when the knock would come on their doors and they too would be arrested, were encouraged by Paul's example. "If Paul can do it, so can we," I can hear them say, and they preached with even more courage.

It's an example of the trickle-down effect of godly leadership and commitment: people encouraged by watching a devout life. And so the gospel is advanced.

Paul did not lash out in bitterness at those who put him in prison; he knew clearly he was there because he preached the gospel. And he knew God would use even those awful circumstances for His glory.

Now, how about your circumstances? You may be pretty miserable, but can you say, "What has happened to me has really served to advance the gospel"?

TAKE A BREATH

Offer your circumstances to the Lord. Then see what He does with them—for His glory.

Here is my life, Lord Jesus.
Use it to build Your kingdom.

WHAT CAN YOU SEE?

If you ever watched one of those documentaries on TV about the riches of ancient Egypt, you were no doubt amazed at the priceless treasures that were used to bury the pharaohs.

For instance, King Tutankhamun ("King Tut" to most of us) was buried in an immense yellow quartzite sarcophagus that took the efforts of several men to move. Inside were three elaborate coffins, the first two of beautifully carved wood with colorful blue and red glass inlays. The final coffin, however, was made of solid gold nearly an inch thick. The famous mask that was at the head of the coffin is now considered to be the greatest Egyptian work of art in history. The total value is so great that it can't even be determined. And King Tut was a mere boy king who ruled only about ten years!

Moses, who was raised as the son of a pharaoh's daughter, grew up around riches like these. He was in line to inherit his adopted grandfather's vast wealth. A future of luxury stretched out before him. Yet he turned his back on all these treasures. He gave them up to follow the true God instead of the gods of Egypt. Hebrews 11:26 tells us, "He regarded disgrace for the sake of Christ as of greater value than the treasures of Egypt, because he was looking ahead to his reward."

What foresight Moses had! Right in front of him was the great wealth that could be his, but by faith he also saw the reward that would be his for obeying God. Verse 25 tells us, "He chose to be mistreated along with the people of God rather than to enjoy the pleasures of sin for a short time."

When Moses turned his back on Egypt's riches and identified with the Israelites, he had no idea what the future would hold for him. The best he could hope for was persecution and abuse. Little did he know that eventually he would be used by God to lead the Israelites out of Egypt to the Promised Land. He merely chose God.

And what kept him going? Verse 27 (NLT) gives us his secret: "Moses kept right on going because he kept his eyes on the one who is invisible."

It's so easy to make a decision to follow God, and then as time goes by to let your vision of Him fade. While you're on this earth, you can't see God physically. Everyday material things are right in front of your nose—the beautiful house you'd like some day to own, that handsome guy you want to marry, the prestigious education you want for your children, the fantasy vacation you hope some day to take. The list goes on and on, and it's different for each of us. All these things can very easily become more real to us than God is.

In your life, what are you focusing on? What can you

see? Your spiritual vision will affect the choices you make.

Who knows how God will use you if your vision is focused on Him!

Moses' life was kept on track by focusing on two things:

- The God he could not see, except by faith
- Rewards he could not see, because they would come not in this life but in eternity

We're all so easily distracted. Our lives are full of demands and circumstances that require our attention, and all too often, God slips quietly into the background of our thoughts.

Remember the mission statement we discussed back on page 59? I suggested keeping it posted where you would be constantly reminded of your number-one priority. You may want to add a couple of things to your mission statement now: first, a reminder that all you do is done for God, and second, that the rewards you are working toward are eternal rather than earthly.

Invisible and eternal Lord,
be more real to me than all that is visible and earthly.

Sign Here

I find that a sticky note makes a great Bible marker. I like to put one on the verse where I want to start reading the next time I pick up my Bible. The one I'm using right now has one of those arrows that says, "Sign here." I hadn't really given it a thought until I noticed that today it points at Ephesians 6:6–7 (NLT): "Do the will of God with all your heart. Work with enthusiasm, as though you were working for the Lord rather than for people."

And the marker says, "Sign here." Am I willing to do that? Or is doing God's will wholeheartedly something I tend to think of doing in the future but not in common, ordinary "today."

Take a look at your day. It's probably nothing special. Pretty routine. In fact, in all probability it's filled with activities that are similar to what you did yesterday. Sometimes it's hard to think you're working for the Lord when you're changing a baby's diaper, or shopping at the market, or planning the sales event for the company where you work. Yet in doing the mundane, ordinary tasks, it's your attitude that makes all the difference in the world.

Working with all your heart means washing the sticky

floor *again*. Answering a five-year-old's questions *again*.
Going to the same old job *again*. But this time, doing those
tasks with a sense of purpose—from the heart, for the Lord.

Sometimes people think that if they could only work
for a Christian organization, they'd *really* be working for the
Lord. Or if they were only missionaries or pastors—now, that
would make them truly valuable to God, because those jobs
are really important. But if God's will is for you to be a full-
time mom or an office manager, or to let your light shine as a
waitress in a restaurant, then what is most significant for you
is to do your daily tasks with all your heart—as though you
were doing them directly for the Lord.

A well-known song says, "In my life, Lord, be glorified"
—and the last line adds the word "today." You know, today
is really the only day we have. Do you want to do God's will
from the heart today—with all your heart? Then "Sign here."

TAKE A BREATH

How can you commit yourself to glorifying God?

Try using the power of your imagination. Children are
good at make-believe, but as adults we've often forgotten
this mental skill. The next time, you're doing a tedious
chore, though, you can use your imagination to catch a
glimpse of what's truly real. As you scrub the kitchen floor,
imagine that Jesus will walk across it; as you prepare a
report at work, imagine that Jesus will review it; as you do
the family laundry, imagine that Jesus will wear the clean

clothes. This is no make-believe game—when we offer each thing we do as service to Jesus, even the smallest, most mundane task becomes holy.

Jesus, I offer to You each thing that I do.
May my every action please You.

Train Yourself
to Be Godly

I hate exercising. I really do. It takes too much time and it's—well, boring! But thanks to my daughter's nagging, I'm finally convinced it's a necessity if I'm going to maintain my health and strength. Otherwise, my body won't hold up to what I feel the Lord wants me to do.

Have you ever noticed what Paul says about exercise in 1 Timothy 4:7–8? "Train yourself to be godly. . .physical training is of some value, but godliness has value for all things. . .the present life and the life to come."

Physical fitness involves three elements: stretching, weights, and aerobics. If we don't stretch (even though it's a *bore!*), our muscles shorten, and we become stiff. It takes working out with weights to build strong bones and increase muscle strength. (Ugh! That's hard work!) Aerobic exercise strengthens the heart muscles and lung capacity. (But it takes so much time!)

I never cease to be amazed at how lazy I am. And it's easy to be spiritually lazy as well. Godly fitness also involves those same three elements—

- stretching my limits

- working with weights that are nearly too heavy

- running toward the goal of laying hold of that for which God laid hold of me (Philippians 3:12).

I often tell women that God doesn't ask you to do anything He doesn't equip you to do. His calling is in line with the talents, personality, and spiritual gifts He gives you, so you don't have to be afraid of God's will for your life. But I always have to add that He usually stretches us to the limits within those parameters. Don't be surprised when God stretches your spiritual "tendons." That's what lengthens your reach.

The metaphor goes even further, for the weights in life often progress from light to heavier as you go along. But God has promised not to give you more than you can bear. You can trust Him to know your limits.

Don't stop short of laying hold of God's purpose for you. Push on. He has created you for a purpose, and your efforts to lay hold of that purpose will only make you stronger in the Lord.

TAKE A BREATH

Two more elements are part of fitness, whether it's physical or spiritual: good nutrition and rest. Spiritually, I need to feed my soul and spend time resting in God's presence—

parts I'm tempted to leave undone because I don't *feel* like I'm doing anything when I'm resting in the Lord. *Doing* something seems so much more profitable.

Do you need to resolve today, with God's help, to be more physically fit? Even more important, says Paul, is training to be spiritually fit. Stop for a moment and ask God what changes He wants you to make.

Make me strong, loving Lord,
so that I may serve You well all the days of my life.

WHEN TOUGH TIMES COME

Inspiration for Days

When You Feel Like Quitting

I Will Not Forget You

Sometimes God allows a long period of pain and hardship in our lives, and we begin to wonder if He really cares. "He must have given up on me," we think. "Perhaps among all the billions of people of the world He has to keep track of, He has forgotten me—or worse yet, forsaken me." And that's a scary feeling!

That's exactly how the children of Israel felt, for they said, "The Lord has forsaken me, the Lord has forgotten me" (Isaiah 49:14). With our human limitations, perhaps this is the only way we can explain to ourselves why God doesn't rescue us out of trouble. After all, we know He is almighty. So if we don't sense that He is present with us, and we don't see Him saving us from our dilemma, we just assume He has forgotten us and given up on us.

But look at what God says in reply when we feel this way: "Can a mother forget the baby at her breast and have no compassion on the child she has borne? Though she may forget, I will not forget you!" (Isaiah 49:15).

What a comparison! No mother—not even the one who has given up her baby for adoption—ever forgets the child she has borne. Even those who have aborted a baby in the early months of pregnancy never forget. Yet God says, though a mother may forget, "I will not forget you!" What a strong picture of His love!

Then He adds one more phrase for emphasis: "See, I have written your name on my hand" (verse 16 NLT). When elementary school kids get a crush on a girlfriend or boyfriend, they often write their initials on their hand. It's a semi-secret way of identifying with that person.

But God in the person of Jesus Christ has more than our names written on His hands. He has nail prints on those hands to prove His love for us! He suffered far more than the pangs of childbirth to make us His children. His pain—the pain of death on a cross—left scars that will forever be a reminder of His love.

"Greater love has no one than this," said Jesus, "that he lay down his life for his friends" (John 15:13). Jesus did just that for you. You can be sure that the One who died for you will never forget you or forsake you. Never!

TAKE A BREATH

When you feel as though God has forgotten you, reread Isaiah 49:14–15. Then imagine Christ's scarred hands with *your* name written across the palms.

Thank You, Jesus, for bearing me. . .
for remembering me. . .for loving me.

You Lift Up My Head

If you're like me, sometimes you wake up in the morning thinking, "I don't even feel like getting out of bed today—I just don't want to face life." We think that way when we don't want to deal with issues we know the day will bring. We're tired of the battle.

David felt that way. And not without reason. He tells about it in Psalm 3. His son Absalom was trying to kill him so that Absalom could become king in his father's place; David was having to run from his own son. What's more, people were telling him there was no hope even in God. "Many are saying of me, 'God will not deliver him'" (verse 2). "It's no use, David, there's no chance you'll survive," they told him.

All the circumstances looked bad. David knew that as soon as morning came, he had to be on the run again, looking for a new hiding place—where his own son couldn't find him!

But David didn't listen to those who were discouraging him, and he didn't give up. He felt like throwing in the towel, but he didn't. No, in his heart-of-hearts he knew that what they were saying was not true, and He reminded God of that truth. Here are his exact words: "But you are a shield around me, O Lord; you bestow glory on me and lift up my head" (verse 3).

Do you need a good dose of encouragement? Does your head need "lifting up"? David knew that human help was not enough. "From the Lord comes deliverance," he said (verse 8). He didn't count on his own cleverness or ingenuity. He didn't count on his friends or his soldiers. He knew that his protection and his deliverance would come from God.

From the Lord comes deliverance from enemies—and from discouragement.

TAKE A BREATH

The next time your head needs "lifting up," take a few minutes to do a mini Bible study. All the following verses are in the book of Psalms, so they're easy to find.

Lift up to the Lord:

- your eyes (Psalm 121:1; 123:1)

- your voice (Psalm 142:1–2)

- your hands (Psalm 28:2; 134:2)

- your soul (Psalm 25:1; 86:4; 143:8)

The five or ten minutes of reading are well worth the time. If you do those four things, I can pretty much guarantee that God will "lift up your head"—yes, He will bring encouragement and fresh inspiration to your heart. I know, because He does it for me.

When my head hangs, Lord, I see only my own stumbling feet.
But when You lift my head, I look into Your face—
no wonder I am encouraged!

Joy in Hard Times

Incredible! Just look at these two attitudes Peter tells us to have when we run smack-dab into difficult times:

1. Don't be surprised. (I always am!)
2. Be very glad. (I never am!)

You can read it for yourself:

Dear friends, don't be surprised at the fiery trials you are going through, as if something strange were happening to you. Instead, be very glad—because these trials will make you partners with Christ in his suffering, and afterward you will have the wonderful joy of sharing his glory when it is displayed to all the world. (1 Peter 4:12–13 NLT)

These verses tell me that trials are normal, not unusual. I always think life should go along smoothly, and it sometimes does for a while. But sooner or later (usually sooner than later), a problem comes along—an illness, a financial need, a personal criticism, or whatever—and it hits me between the eyes. I'm *always* surprised.

But being "very glad" in the middle of trials is even more foreign to me than not being surprised by them. (My thesaurus gives the word *celebrate* as a synonym for "be glad" or "rejoice"—can you believe it?)

I'm glad Peter didn't say we're to be glad *because of* our trials. No, we're to be glad *in* them, because through suffering we're partners with Christ in His suffering. I don't exactly know what that means, but Peter wasn't the only one who said it. Paul also talked about "the fellowship of sharing in his sufferings, becoming like him in his death" (Philippians 3:10). It certainly speaks of a close relationship—and I can rejoice in that. Closeness to the One who cared enough to die for me!

Don't forget that last phrase where Peter tells us that after the suffering is over, we'll have wonderful joy—we'll be ecstatic—when His glory is revealed at the culmination of events when He returns. I don't know all that entails either, but it sounds absolutely fascinating.

In the meantime, the Bible promises if we suffer, He will comfort us. Yes, our heavenly Father is the "Father of compassion and the God of all comfort, who comforts us in all our troubles" (2 Corinthians 1:3–4). What's more, we'll be able to comfort others with the same comfort that God uses to comfort us.

You may feel that suffering is raining down on your

life right now. Paul said that would happen. But the more we suffer, "the more God will shower us with his comfort through Christ" (2 Corinthians 1:5 NLT). Be encouraged that God is going to let His comfort overflow from your life to the lives of others.

And that's reason for joy—especially in tough times!

TAKE A BREATH

How can you be glad when everything seems to be going wrong? It all depends on how much you believe you can trust God. If you *know*, deep down in the bottom of your heart, that God will never forget you, that He will always take care of you, and most of all, that He truly loves you, then you will not worry about today's storms—because you will be confident that new life will come from the rain, and tomorrow the sun will shine.

So how do we get that sort of confidence? By getting to know the God we love. The darker the days, the more we need to spend time in His presence. When we do, He will fill our hearts with comfort—and yes, even gladness.

I don't feel like celebrating, Lord.
Please draw my heart closer to Yours.
Share with me Your comfort and joy.

WHY?

"Why did God let this happen?" our hearts cry out when we face tragedy.

A baby is born with severe birth defects. A young college graduate with all of life ahead of him is killed by a drunk driver. A mother of three small children dies unexpectedly in surgery. Why?

There is no magic formula that always "works" with God. He doesn't deal with every situation the same way. Sometimes for a short period of time He allows us to be in frightening situations and then quickly answers our prayers and takes us out of the dark circumstances. I like those answers! Other times, He lets us struggle with pain and heartache all the way from beginning to end; only afterward can we see how our faith has grown as a result. But what about the times when we can see no good whatsoever in what has happened?

Well, for one thing, we have to remember that we don't know *everything*. Our knowledge is very limited compared to God's knowledge. How much do you think you know of all the information that exists in our world? Ten percent? Or maybe only one percent? Is it possible that God has good reasons for what He has allowed, reasons that exist outside the realm of your understanding? I'm sure we'd all have to admit that's more than likely.

Here's another thought—and I think it's the secret. Paul says, "We do not want you to be uninformed, brothers, about the hardships we suffered. . . . This happened that we might not rely on ourselves but on God" (2 Corinthians 1:8–9).

When we can understand why we're facing hard times, we don't have to rely on Him; we can figure it out for ourselves. We say, "Sure, this is terrible, but I can see what God is doing through this awful situation."

But when we can't see any good whatever that is being accomplished, we have nothing left to do but to trust God in faith. In fact, I'm not sure anything else is truly faith, for, as Philip Yancey writes, "Faith *requires* obedience without full knowledge."[10]

When we cannot understand, we can rely on God. "Let him who walks in the dark, who has no light, trust in the name of the LORD and rely on his God" (Isaiah 50:10).

And God *is* reliable—that is, He has qualities that merit our confidence or trust. He is dependable, secure, tried and true, trustworthy, infallible, unerring, attested, authenticated, circumstantiated, confirmed, proven, verified, unimpeachable, unquestionable. And that's only a tiny part of the list that describes God!

Do you feel as though you're stumbling around in the dark?

No one likes to walk in the dark. We somehow feel that things aren't right if we can't see where we're going, that we *deserve* to see the road ahead. But it doesn't take faith to walk confidently in the bright sunlight of noon. In times like that, we can rely on our own intelligence and abilities. Faith comes into play, however, when we walk forward through pitch darkness, relying totally on the grasp of God's hand on ours for guidance.

When you can't understand the circumstances, the best thing you can say is, "I don't know why, but I know God!" And I'm going to believe that "He cares for those who trust in him" (Nahum 1:7).

I can't see the path I should take, Lord—
so I'm putting my hand in Yours. Please don't let me fall.

Shelter in
the Time of Storm

Bad news—I don't like it! It is often overwhelming and brings pain. That's why I wake with a start when the phone rings in the middle of the night. Or I tense up when I hear about a plane crash on a day my husband is flying.

We really can't help it that the adrenaline kicks in when we hear bad news, for our bodies are made to prepare for "flight or fight" at a moment's notice. That's a natural reaction. But we can deal with the fear that comes.

The psalmist says that the secret is a steadfast and secure heart. "He will have no fear of bad news," the psalmist writes. "His heart is steadfast, trusting in the LORD. His heart is secure, he will have no fear; in the end he will look in triumph on his foes" (112:7–8).

That sounds great, but how do you get a steadfast, trusting heart that has no fear? I don't know about you, but I wasn't born with one!

I like to think about it this way: Bad news is like a storm that rises quickly on the ocean of our lives and would sink our ship if we didn't do something quickly. When the storm comes, we need a harbor where we can drop anchor. "I would hurry to my place of shelter, far from the tempest and storm," says the psalmist (55:8).

A steadfast heart is simply one who has run to the Lord for shelter. The reason that your fear is dispelled is that you are trusting in the Lord. You know God is your source of wisdom, strength, and safekeeping. And when you trust Him, your heart is secure.

You see, it's all about God and not about us. You and I are fragile and easily broken. But when bad news comes, God is a strong harbor where you can put down the anchor of your heart.

As Psalm 112 says, "In the end" I know I will be able not only to survive but to overcome.

TAKE A BREATH

When bad news comes, make a habit of turning to God before you do anything else. When your heart is close to His, you will be more able to deal with whatever comes next.

I have anchored my heart in Your harbor, Lord.
Keep me safe.

GOD'S STRONG ARMS

When I first read that familiar writing called "Footprints in the Sand," the message deeply touched my heart.

> One night I dreamed I was walking along the beach
>   with the Lord.
> Many scenes from my life flashed across the sky.
> In each scene I noticed footprints in the sand.
> Sometimes there were two sets of footprints.
> Other times there was one set of footprints.
> This bothered me because I noticed that during the
>   low periods of my life
> When I was suffering from anguish, sorrow, or
>   defeat,
> I could see only one set of footprints.
> So I said to the Lord, "You promised me, Lord,
> That if I followed you, you would walk with me
>   always.
> But I noticed that during the most trying periods of
>   my life
> There have only been one set of prints in the sand.

Why, when I have needed you most,
Have you not been there for me?"
The Lord replied,
"The times when you have seen only one set of
    footprints
Is when I carried you."[11]

That's wonderful! I thought. *God carries me when the
going gets tough, just as I would pick up my own child and
carry him over rough ground.*

But then a nagging thought tugged at my enthusiasm:
*I wonder if it's really true. It sounds nice, but like so many
syrupy writings that have no basis in scripture, maybe this isn't
founded on biblical truth. Does God really carry me when the
going gets tough?*

I was excited when I found Deuteronomy 1:31: "There
you saw how the LORD your God carried you, as a father
carries his son, all the way you went until you reached this
place."

Wow, it's true! He really does carry us!

Notice the event this verse comes from. The children
of Israel were right up to the border of the Promised Land
with their toes practically hanging over the edge, but they
were getting cold feet about taking the land as their own.
At that point of decision, Moses reminded them that all
across the desert from Egypt to this place God had carried
them. Three long years! A God who would do that was

strong enough to give them the land He had promised. He would not forsake them now that they were ready to take possession.

As additional confirmation of this encouraging thought, I found more verses that speak of God carrying us. Take a look:

> He will feed his flock like a shepherd. He will carry the lambs in his arms, holding them close to his heart. He will gently lead the mother sheep with their young. (Isaiah 40:11 NLT)

Isaiah 46:3 confirms the same thought: "Listen to me, O house of Jacob, . . .you whom I have upheld since you were conceived, and have carried since your birth."

No, God will never forsake me:

> The LORD himself goes before you and will be with you; he will never leave you nor forsake you. Do not be afraid; do not be discouraged. (Deuteronomy 31:8)

I can count on God to walk with me—always. And when life brings more than I can handle and I am about to stumble and fall, I can count on His strong arms to carry me. It's in the Bible!

TAKE A BREATH

When doubts fill your mind, turn to scripture. Your faith
will be bolstered by the promises you find there.

Loving God, when my legs are too weak to walk,
please carry me.

WHAT GOOD
COMES FROM SUFFERING?

My friend Juanita suffered terribly with cancer of the face. She lost one eye and part of her jaw to that horrible disease. For twelve years, she fought the battle to stay ahead of its advance. Why? What possible good could come from what she endured?

If you think I'm going to give you the full answer in the next four hundred words, you'll be disappointed. I don't think we will have the whole answer to questions like this until we are in the presence of the Lord. But I did find two verses in the Bible that tell me suffering is not wasted.

Isaiah 38:17 and 15 (NLT):

Yes, it was good for me to suffer this anguish. Now I will walk humbly throughout my years because of this anguish I have felt.

If nothing else, suffering refines and perfects us. I could see that in Juanita's life. Her faith and trust in the Lord were an inspiration to all who watched her go through this terrible ordeal. She was a shining example of someone who "fought the good fight of faith," all the time trusting that God knew what He was doing in her life, even if she didn't.

One of the good things suffering often brings is a closer relationship with the Lord. Joni Eareckson Tada, who was left a quadriplegic after a diving accident in her teen years, says that sometimes people come to her today and say, "Joni, I wish I had your relationship with God." But, Joni says, no one wants her suffering. Yet it was through the suffering that she developed closeness with the Lord.

I don't like pain! At the dentist's office, I want to know my tooth is thoroughly, totally, 100 percent numb before I see the drill advancing toward my mouth. That's probably normal—part of the instinct for survival. But as Rick Warren says, "God cares more about my character than my comfort." If He thinks pain will draw me to Himself, He will use even that unwanted tool to bring about my ultimate good.

Only eternity will reveal the full explanation for suffering. Paul says, "All that I know now is partial and incomplete, but then I will know everything completely, just as God knows me now" (1 Corinthians 13:12 NLT). In the meantime, in the middle of his suffering, Paul declared, "I know the one in whom I trust, and I am sure that he is able to guard what I have entrusted to him until the day of his return" (2 Timothy 1:12 NLT).

I don't know why Juanita had to go through such

intense suffering. But I do know that the presence of Jesus was evident in her life through all the pain.

Her life articulated to all who watched her how suffering can draw one closer to the Lord. Her experience with God spoke volumes about trusting God when you don't know the reasons for what He is doing.

TAKE A BREATH

Next time you're in pain (whether physical or emotional), instead of asking, "Why?" try asking God to draw you closer to Him in the midst of the suffering. The presence of God can bring you new life.

In the midst of my pain, God, draw me close to You.

Close to the
Brokenhearted

You feel absolutely crushed. Perhaps someone you love very much has turned his back on you and rejected you. Maybe you just learned that a family member has died. Or perhaps you are processing a doctor's report that says you have a deadly disease. You are grief-stricken—heartbroken—knowing you have turned a corner in life that means nothing will ever be the same again.

You picked up this book, looking for some word of comfort or encouragement. While there is nothing I can say that will take away your pain, I can assure you of one thing: "The LORD is close to the brokenhearted." You find that truth in Psalm 34:18.

To have God close in such a time as you are experiencing is the greatest comfort you can have. He is close enough to hold you tight to Himself when you feel you can't go on another moment. He is close enough to console you as no one on earth can do. He is close enough to strengthen you and guide you during the darkness of the hours that lie ahead.

One of the very reasons Jesus came to this earth two

thousand years ago was to bring comfort. When He visited the synagogue in Nazareth and stood up to read scripture, He was handed the book of Isaiah. Although at that time there were no chapter divisions, Jesus turned to what is our Isaiah 61 and began to read:

> The Spirit of the LORD is upon Me,
> Because He has anointed Me
> > to preach the gospel to the poor;
> He has sent Me to heal the brokenhearted. . . .

After finishing the passage, Jesus closed the book, gave it back to the attendant, and sat down. All eyes in the synagogue were fixed on Him. Then He said, "Today this Scripture is fulfilled in your hearing" (from Luke 4:18–21 NKJV).

Yes, Jesus was sent to heal the brokenhearted. He "saves those who are crushed in spirit." "He heals the brokenhearted and binds up their wounds" (Psalm 34:18; 147:3).

I encourage you to call out to God as never before, for "The LORD is close to all who call on him" (Psalm 145:18 NLT). "As a mother comforts her child, so will I comfort you," God promises (Isaiah 66:13).

You may be thinking, "All that you have done, Darlene, is quote scripture in this selection." Yes, that's true. But when the bottom has fallen out for you in life and everything is gone, the only thing that will help is for you to realize you still have God. It's His Word—His promises—that will hold you firm as the waves of sorrow and heartache sweep down on you.

Dear friend, through all your pain, hold tight to Him, and trust Him that some day you will be able to say with the writer of Psalms, "When doubts filled my mind, your comfort gave me renewed hope and cheer" (Psalm 94:19 NLT).

One day you will even be able to comfort others with the way God has brought you through this terribly difficult time. That's in God's Word, too: "He comforts us in all our troubles so that we can comfort others. When others are troubled, we will be able to give them the same comfort God has given us" (2 Corinthians 1:4 NLT).

Just you wait and see!

TAKE A BREATH

Pain demands our attention. But look around. Is there someone in your life who is also suffering and needs comfort? You may be surprised to find that as you pass comfort on to another, you will experience that same comfort yourself. We can form a chain of love, each linked to the other; when we do, we will experience God's love and comfort flowing through us—and find purpose for our pain.

Help me, Lord, to see past my pain to the needs of others.

WHEN YOU
WANT TO
KNOW GOD
BETTER

Inspiration to Have
a Closer Relationship

THE HEAVENS DECLARE. . .

"The heavens declare the glory of God," says Psalm 19:1. It's hard to define the *glory of God*, but we can look at what the heavens declare and get some idea.

First, the heavens declare something of His *dimension*. Not only are the heavens so vast that we don't yet know how large they are, we are told they are still expanding. We can see out only to the distance from which light has reached us since the universe began—that's the observable universe. Who knows what exists beyond what we can observe? If you add to that thought the logical deduction that God has to be greater than the size of His handiwork, you begin to grasp some idea of the dimension of God.

In addition, the heavens declare His *power and intelligence*. They are so vast, yet they are so orderly. Anyone who could create something so immense and yet so organized must be so far greater than us that we will never fully comprehend Him. He is bigger than even our thoughts of Him.

The heavens also declare His *ability to create* beauty. Who hasn't looked up into the sky and marveled at the beauty of the clouds or the stars or the moon. In a *Dennis the Menace* cartoon, Dennis and his friend are staring up in amazement one night at the starry sky above. Awed by what he sees, Dennis comments, "If Heaven is so beautiful underneath, think what it must be like on top!"

The heavens also tell us of His *care* for us, for the heavens give us appropriate light for both day and night. In addition they give us fixed points to help us find our way, to say nothing of the moon's beneficial effect on the tides of our oceans.

And what about God's *precision*? The earth rotates in a 292-million-mile-long orbit around the sun. This takes precisely 365 days, 5 hours, 48 minutes, and 45.51 seconds, accurate to a thousandth of a second! And that's just the accuracy of *one* heavenly body. Can you imagine what collisions would occur in the heavens if God were not a God of precision?

We will probably never fully comprehend the glory of God. But the heavens He created tell us enough that we can know He's big enough to handle any problem we may bring to Him.

TAKE A BREATH

Have you talked to God today about your needs? Philippians 4:6 (NLT) says, "Don't worry about anything; instead, pray about everything. Tell God what you need, and thank him for all he has done." That's an invitation from the same God who

made those amazing heavens. Take a few minutes right now
to talk to Someone who can make a difference!

My mind is too small to comprehend Your glory, God.
But I don't have to understand You to love You.

FINDING GOD

I hate wasting time and energy. If I can see that a project isn't going to work, I want out. Why spin my wheels and not get anywhere?

That's why it's so encouraging to me that when it comes to my relationship with God, He says that if I seek Him, I will find Him. Those exact words are found in 1 Chronicles 28:9 (NLT): "If you seek him, you will find him." No time and energy wasted there. No frustration.

When you think about that straightforward promise, it's absolutely amazing. God is more than the CEO of the universe. He is the supreme being of all creation. He is the most important "person" in existence. How amazing it is to know that as great as He is, I can find Him. Puny, ordinary, unimportant *me* can find God.

I can send an e-mail to the president or to the king, queen, or leader of any nation in the world. But I know before I write that I'll probably get only a form-letter reply—at best. But with God, the creator of the universe, I can have genuine, heart-to-heart communication. What a privilege!

One of the best things about communication with God is that God doesn't care how you speak to Him. The simplest prayer reaches His ears. The grammar doesn't have to be correct. In fact, we don't even need to use words. You probably remember the verse that tells us: "The Holy Spirit helps us in our distress. For we don't even know what we should pray for, nor how we should pray. But the Holy Spirit prays for us with groanings that cannot be expressed in words" (Romans 8:26 NLT). He never puts up a "Closed for the Day" sign, never takes a holiday, never even sleeps. He promises that our heart cries will reach His ear.

Sometimes the Lord and I talk over a cup of tea. Other times I'm on my knees desperately calling out to Him. In the middle of the night, talking to Him calms my nonstop mind.

"Let us come boldly to the throne of our gracious God," advises the writer of Hebrews. "There we will receive his mercy, and we will find grace to help us when we need it" (Hebrews 4:16 NLT). God promises that if we seek Him, we will find Him. We can have free access to the King of kings and Lord of lords and stay with Him as long as we wish.

Why don't we do it more often?

TAKE A BREATH

If you never spoke with a close friend, pretty soon you wouldn't feel as close to her. Oh, you would still care about her, but the events and constant changes of life would come between you. You would no longer share your hearts' concerns, and gradually you would grow apart.

The same is true of our relationship with God. The only

way to be close to Him is to spend time with Him. All we have to do is speak to Him. His line is never busy.

Thank You, Lord, for listening to my smallest worries,
my biggest fears, my grandest joys, my tiniest pleasures.
I'm so glad I can share my life with You.

Knowing God

You've probably met someone who seems to know everybody who is anybody, from film actors to political bigwigs. "Yes, I know the ambassador well. As a matter of fact, the two of us had lunch with the president last week." As unappealing as it is, name-dropping is a common way of getting attention.

Jeremiah says wise men may boast of their wisdom, strong men may brag about their strength, and a wealthy man may show off his riches. But if a person wants to boast, only one thing is worth boasting about: "Let him who boasts boast about this: that he understands and knows me" (see Jeremiah 9:23–24).

Actually, when a person boasts about her wisdom or strength or riches, she is taking credit for what God has given her. She couldn't be wise, strong, or rich without God allowing it. Paul says in 1 Corinthians 4:7 (NLT), "What makes you better than anyone else? What do you have that God hasn't given you? And if all you have is from God, why boast as though you have accomplished something on your own?" That pretty much reduces our right to brag to zero.

But understanding and knowing God?

J. I. Packer wrote a classic book called *Knowing God* that has blessed and challenged many. I think even the title is fascinating. That the God who never had a beginning, the One who made all things out of nothing, is knowable by the human beings He created is amazing to me. That He wants fellowship with me is astounding. Yet scripture says God is the One who "invited you into this wonderful friendship with his Son, Jesus Christ our Lord" (1 Corinthians 1:9 NLT).

A young woman in her mid-twenties wrote in her diary: "I thought this morning how I knew more about my dog Ginger than I know about God. How dreadful to know more about a dog than God!"[12]

How about starting right now to get to know God better.

TAKE A BREATH

Not sure how to begin? You can get under way by taking a Bible concordance (you probably have one in the back of your Bible) and looking up one of the characteristics of God, such as His love, justice, or faithfulness. From the scripture verses listed there, write down what you learn about God. You are sure to be amazed.

Then take a few moments to think about what you learned. What does this tell me about my relationship with God? How does this affect my life?

One last step: Talk to God about what you discovered. Ask Him to reveal Himself to you even more and help you to understand who He is and what He has written. After all, you're talking to the author of the Book!

Reveal Yourself to me through Your Word, dear God.
I want to know You better.

How Big Is God?

I love to look at pictures of the Himalayas—mountains so enormous in size that they take my breath away. The adjective that immediately comes to mind is *awesome*, a word that has the synonyms "overwhelming, grand, splendid, tremendous, remarkable, amazing, awe-inspiring, and astounding." Although I've never actually seen the Himalayas, I'm sure that in "real life" those mighty mountains are all that and more.

But how would you describe God? I think that those same adjectives are about as close as we can come. He is so "awesome" that words fail us to express His greatness.

In Isaiah 57:15, God gives us a description of Himself and where He lives: "For this is what the high and lofty One says—he who lives forever, whose name is holy: 'I live in a high and holy place.'" That is so far above where I live that I feel like a tiny ant in comparison.

But the part I like best is the rest of that verse. Yes, God lives in a high and holy place, "But also with him who is contrite and lowly in spirit, to revive the spirit of the lowly and to revive the heart of the contrite." God's name is holy, but He also stoops to live with anyone who is humble and repentant. He is so big that He can cover all the bases—from the borders of the universe (wherever *they* are) to the tiny dot on the earth where I live. Isaiah goes on to say that He can reach down and revive me when I feel like quitting. This great God can breathe new life into my tired spirit, renewing and revitalizing me.

Country music writer Stuart Hamblen's song "How Big Is God?" puts it well:

He's big enough to rule the mighty universe,
Yet small enough to live within my heart.

That thought helps me put my situation in perspective. The problem I'm struggling with is pretty small in compari-son with Mt. Everest—and God! When I realize this awe-some God truly lives in my heart, I realize I can talk to Him about my needs and know that He will never let me down.

TAKE A BREATH

Make time in your life for moments of awe. When we're so busy with the pressing daily concerns of everyday life, we have little room in our minds and hearts for wonder. No matter how overwhelming your responsibilities, take a moment to look up at a starry sky. . .to watch the sun rise. . .to gaze at your sleeping baby. . .to listen to music that stirs your heart. Times like those create a cathedral space in your heart, soaring moments when God's awesome might will renew your weary heart.

Thank You, awesome Lord,
that You live in the farthest reaches of the universe. . .
and the smallest nook of my heart.

CREATION AND
THE CROSS

When I look at the world about me, I stand in awe of God's handiwork.

Once as I stood in total darkness on a remote island, I looked up and caught my breath as I saw more stars than I ever dreamed existed. My God made those stars!

I stood at the foot of mighty snow-capped mountains and, staring up, felt dwarfed by their dizzying heights and massive dimension. My God made those mountains!

I stood amid acres of spring flowers where hyacinths wafted their sweet fragrance and deep-throated tulips were a feast for the eye with their rainbow colors and waxy petals. My God created those flowers!

But when I stood on a hill called Calvary and, in my mind's eye, saw a wooden cross on which my Savior died for me, I could only bow in wonder. How *could* God send His only Son from the glories of heaven—from closeness to His side—to such an awful death? He gave me only one answer: "I loved the world so much that I gave. . . ."

Creation was easy compared to this! He *spoke* the

stars, the mountains, and the flowers into existence. But words—even the words of Almighty God—were not enough to wash away my sins. God loved, and God gave, and God suffered in my place that I might be clean and pure enough to spend eternity with Him. He paid the price that I might be forgiven. All this He did for me. . . and for you.

Have you responded to God's supreme act of love?

The Bible says, "If you confess with your mouth, 'Jesus is Lord,' and believe in your heart that God raised him from the dead, you will be saved. For it is with your heart that you believe and are justified, and it is with your mouth that you confess and are saved" (Romans 10:9–10). At that point you become His child.

Perhaps you are already God's child, but you're challenged when you think of what it cost God for you to be in His family. Second Corinthians 5:15 (NLT) says, "He died for everyone so that those who receive his new life will no longer live to please themselves. Instead, they will live to please Christ, who died and was raised for them."

When He loves us so much, what else can we do but give Him our lives?

TAKE A BREATH

Whether right now you're taking that first step of placing your faith in God's sacrifice for you, or you're responding by making a deeper commitment to live for God instead of for yourself, focus on His love for you. Make this your prayer: "All this You did for me! What can I do for You?"

Jesus, You loved me enough to give me everything, even Your life. Please take my life in return. Use me as You want.

A Democracy
or a Kingdom?

The author and preacher A. W. Tozer had a way of saying things! In his book *The Divine Conquest* he pointed out that we often treat God "as visiting royalty in a democratic country."[13]

In America, which, of course, is a democracy, we are always pleased and honored to have a king visit from another nation. He is given "the royal treatment." Leaders hold banquets in his honor, feature him on TV, and put his picture in the papers. But as highly as he may be respected and admired, we don't let him change any of our laws. We don't want a king telling us what to do, because this is a democratic country, where decisions are made by the vote of the people.

Tozer went on to say that while people are willing to occasionally mention God's name, and at certain seasons, such as Christmas and Easter, He is celebrated to a degree, usually all this amounts to is the flattery we would give a king who is an honored guest. People still want to rule their own lives.

"As long as man is allowed to play host he will honor God with his attention," says Tozer, "but always he [God] must remain a guest and never seek to be Lord. Man will have it understood that this is his world; he will make its laws and decide how it shall be run. God is permitted to decide nothing. Man bows to him and, as he bows, manages with difficulty to conceal the crown upon his own head."[14]

How true! Our natural inclination is to want our lives to be a democracy, where God and ourselves have equal votes in making choices. Sometimes our prayers go something like this: "Tell me what you want me to do, God." But inside we're thinking, "I have veto power if I don't like it." But God doesn't give us that option. In our lives, either He is on the throne or we are.

Which is it for you? Is your life a democracy or a kingdom? Yes, God wants to be King, the ultimate decision maker, but He is a gentleman and will wait until you place Him on the throne of your life.

TAKE A BREATH

Are you ready to pray, "Your kingdom come, your will be done on earth as it is in heaven" (Matthew 6:10)? This could be the day you truly crown Him King.

Be the ruler, God, of all my life—
from the smallest details to the biggest decisions,
from the moment I wake in the morning
until I close my eyes in sleep. Let me hold nothing back.

TALKING TO GOD

Let's talk about taking time for prayer.

Ooooh—did you feel a twinge of guilt when you read that sentence? We know that we ought to pray, but often we feel guilty because prayer has such a low priority in our lives.

The apostle Peter said praying takes self-control. He wrote, "The end of all things is near. Therefore be clear-minded and self-controlled so that you can pray" (1 Peter 4:7). No doubt God had Peter write that because He knew the closer we got to the end times, the more complicated life would become and the more competition there would be for our time.

Today we have choices of what to do with our time that our grandparents and certainly our great-grandparents never had. More than ever before we're aware not only of the needs of people who are close to us but the needs of people on the other side of the globe as well; the media keeps the whole world "in our face." We feel compelled to action. And prayer doesn't feel like action. Calvin Miller writes, "Christians are prone to ignore times of retreat because ministering seems more important: doing seems better than praying. But prayer is doing."[15] Good point!

I am so easily distracted from prayer. Just checking my e-mail will do it. So will my ringing cell phone. A messy closet calls out for reorganization. A graphic news story glues me to the TV, and before I hardly realize it, a chunk of my time is gone.

While I'm sure that all of us would admit that prayer is important, an old proverb says, "I practice daily what I believe; everything else is religious talk."[16]

Ouch! That means that what I spend my time on is an indication of what I think is important.

Sometimes we think we're so busy that we can skip prayer time. I'm always challenged by Martin Luther's attitude, "I have so many things to do today, I dare not ignore my time with God."[17]

Would you like to have had the opportunity to talk with some of the great names of history? How about Marco Polo or Johann Sebastian Bach or Thomas Edison? Would you jump at the chance? Yes, of course, you would consider it a privilege.

How much greater is the privilege to spend time with the One who created our world and the galaxies beyond!

If I am going to find time to pray, I will have to be, as Peter says, clear-minded and self-controlled. But the trade-off is time spent with the God of eternity, who has unlimited understanding, unlimited power, and unlimited love.

Often when we stop to pray, a jillion thoughts crowd in. During my own prayer time, I have learned I'd better have paper and pencil nearby so I can write down what comes to mind. That way I can leave my distracting thought on the paper, where I can deal with it later and get on with praying.

I'm sure that's why Peter reminded us that two things are necessary to pray:

1. Clear-mindedness. In my case, that means I must literally "clear my mind" to focus on the Lord. I must push aside those pestering thoughts that intrude, in order to quiet my heart before Him.

2. Self-control. This requires saying "Yes" to prayer and saying "No" to other demands on my time because prayer is more important.

Clear my mind, Lord, that I may concentrate on You.

FOR 24/7 LIVING

Inspiration for
Common, Ordinary Days

MAKING DECISIONS
GOD'S WAY

Sometimes you feel perfectly capable of making your own decisions. You know exactly what you want to do. And that is not all bad. After all, God has given human beings a degree of understanding about life. I don't think you have to ask God whether or not to brush your teeth or take a shower. Because God breathed into Adam His own breath, and you're a descendant of Adam, you have a measure of insight and discernment. Job said, "It is the spirit in a man, the breath of the Almighty, that gives him understanding" (32:8). The common sense you have is a gift from God.

Yet having the "breath of the Almighty" in us, we sometimes think we know enough to make *all* our own decisions. And that's where we get into trouble. Understanding belongs to God, says Job: "To God belong wisdom and power; counsel and understanding are his" (12:13). His understanding is infinitely greater than yours or mine. And in most areas of life, we need His direction for our lives.

Because God created life, He is the best source of wisdom. I love the promises for guidance that are found in the Bible:

"I am the LORD your God, who teaches you what is best for you, who directs you in the way you should go." (Isaiah 48:17)

As your words are taught, they give light; even the simple can understand them. (Psalm 119:130 NLT)

The LORD says, "I will guide you along the best pathway for your life. I will advise you and watch over you." (Psalm 32:8 NLT)

God has promised to tell us what we need to do. But once God has told us, the next step is to follow His directions. After Nebuchadnezzar had conquered the people of Judah and taken most of them to Babylon, those who were left in Judah came to the prophet Jeremiah asking him to pray for them. Their leader had just been murdered. They didn't know whether to stay in their homeland or to try to escape to Egypt.

"Beg the LORD your God to show us what to do and where to go," they wisely said (Jeremiah 42:3 NLT). "Whether we like it or not, we will obey the LORD our God to whom we send you with our plea. For if we obey him, everything will turn out well for us" (verse 6). Good for them!

"I will certainly pray to the LORD your God as you have requested," responded Jeremiah (42:4). Ten days later, he called the people together and gave them God's answer: Don't be afraid of the king of Babylon, stay in the land, don't go to Egypt. "Indeed, all who are determined to go to Egypt to settle there will die" (verse 17), he added—just in case they didn't understand the seriousness of God's answer.

"You are lying!" the people responded. "The LORD our God has not sent you to say, 'You must not go to Egypt' " (Jeremiah 43:2). So, all the people made the move to Egypt in disobedience to the Lord. There they began to offer incense to the gods of the Egyptians, and as Jeremiah had warned, disaster and death followed.

It's not enough to ask for God's guidance. We must do what He tells us. Don't let it go to your head that you have "the breath of the Almighty" in you. If we ask Him, God will tell us where we should go and what we should do. Our part, whether it is favorable or unfavorable, is to "obey the LORD our God." Take it from the people of Judah—following God's direction is the best way to go!

TAKE A BREATH

Is there something you know God is asking you to do? Stop asking others for advice, hoping someone will give you a good reason not to do what you know God wants. Don't be like Jonah who had to be swallowed by a great fish before he would accept God's direction. Yield yourself to God. His will for you always leads to life.

Give me the strength, God, to do Your will.

ETERNITY IN OUR HEARTS

It's a bit frustrating that about the time of life when we have accumulated some wisdom and experience, we find that our health and energy to put them to good use seem to start winding down. Caryn Leschen said, "Thirty-five is when you finally get your head together and your body starts falling apart." A. W. Tozer put it more eloquently:

> Life is a short and fevered rehearsal for a concert we cannot stay to give. Just when we appear to have attained some proficiency we are forced to lay our instruments down. There is simply not time enough to think, to become, to perform what the constitution of our natures indicates we are capable of.[18]

Scripture says that God has "set eternity in the hearts of men" (Ecclesiastes 3:11). We have a sense that life goes on beyond what exists on this earth. But we cannot see what is beyond. So we tend to hold on tightly to this life, thinking, *This is all I know.*

The writers of the New Testament often remind us that

life is temporary. Paul compared our bodies to tents. "For we know that when this earthly tent we live in is taken down—when we die and leave these bodies—we will have a home in heaven, an eternal body made for us by God himself and not by human hands" (2 Corinthians 5:1 NLT).

He went on to say, "Our dying bodies make us groan and sigh, but it's not that we want to die and have no bodies at all. We want to slip into our new bodies so that these dying bodies will be swallowed up by everlasting life" (2 Corinthians 5:4 NLT). You're right about that, Paul! Any woman who has lived long enough to feel the creaks and stiffness of aging joints and has seen in the mirror ever-deepening wrinkles looks forward to a new body.

Peter further reminds us, "Dear brothers and sisters, you are foreigners and aliens here" (1 Peter 2:11 NLT). As the old song says, "This world is not my home. I'm just a-travelin' through."

"So we don't look at the troubles we can see right now; rather, we look forward to what we have not yet seen. For the troubles we see will soon be over, but the joys to come will last forever" (2 Corinthians 4:18 NLT). That's the "forever" we sense in our hearts, the awareness of eternity that God has placed there.

I think Tozer is right: This life is only a rehearsal; the concert is yet to come. On that day we will be able to express what right now we can only feel in our hearts. What a day that will be!

TAKE A BREATH

Do you ever feel as though life is slipping away from you? Some days does the passage of time fill you with anxiety? Those feelings are normal, for your heart was made for eternity. When anxious thoughts oppress you, remember: Your home is in heaven. Don't fret over what passes away on this earth. Instead, dwell on that which will last forever.

You are my home, God. Thank You that when all around me changes, including my own body, You remain the same.

God's Gift
of Artistic Skills

Are you artistic? Not me! I'm like my mom. When my son asked her to draw a picture of a dog, she did her best. But he took one look at what she had drawn and said, "Okay, now draw a dog!"

I do love to watch other people fashion lovely things. They seem to be in partnership with God, who created all the marvelous beauty we see in our world.

Take a look at Exodus 28–36, and you'll find some interesting thoughts about artistic skill. These chapters describe how the tent was made for Old Testament worship, along with the clothing and articles to be used in it.

Notice that skill to do the sewing was a gift from the Lord. "Tell all the skilled men to whom I have given wisdom in such matters that they are to make garments" (Exodus 28:3).

I'm fascinated that scripture says the filling of God's Spirit gifted at least one of the men with special artistic skills. Until I noticed this verse, I figured the work of the Holy Spirit in our lives was only for spiritual purposes. Scripture says, however, that "the LORD has chosen Bezalel. . .and he has filled him with the Spirit of God, with skill, ability and knowledge in all kinds of crafts—to make artistic designs. . .and to engage in all kinds of artistic craftsmanship" (Exodus 35:30–33). In the power of the Holy Spirit, Bezalel blessed the children of Israel with his practical abilities.

What a variety of skills God gave these people: expertise in artistic design, sewing, embroidery, weaving, metalwork, and construction, and working with stone, wood, and gems—all kinds of craftsmanship!

He also gave some the ability to teach their skills to others. "He has given both him [Bezalel] and Oholiab. . .the ability to teach others" (Exodus 35:34).

In these chapters, I noticed that there are two parts to being used artistically by God.

- First, recognize that God has given the skill, and
- be willing to do the work (Exodus 36:2).

And what about the rest of us? If we don't have these talents, are we left out? No, if we're not gifted, we can provide for those who are. Exodus 35:29 says, "All the Israelite men and women who were willing brought to the LORD freewill offerings for all the work the LORD through Moses had commanded them to do." Either way, God gets what He wants accomplished—if we are willing.

God is the author of beauty, and those who create

artistic loveliness must feel a distinctive kinship with Him. When you realize that this ability is God's special gift to you, perhaps your gift will seem more precious. Offer to Him everything you create for His glory. In doing so, you will bless those of us who wish we had your talent.

TAKE A BREATH

Do you sew? Thank God for your hands' skill.

Can you draw or paint or sculpt? Thank God for your talent.

Can you write words that move others with their power and beauty? Give God praise for your ability.

Are you good at teaching others? Be grateful to the One who gave you your skill.

Do you cook delicious meals? Bless God who allows you to feed others.

Are you good at cleaning house? Keeping books? Organizing an office? Listening to others? Leading a group? Whatever your ability, God has a place for your skills. He has shared His own creativity and abilities with each one of us. As we use that which we have been given, we build the kingdom of God.

Use my talents, Lord. Do Your work through me.

How You
Can Keep Standing

I love old-fashioned stories because they let me push back the curtains of time and see life as it was in the past. Here is one of those stories.

A minister traveling by train was the only passenger in the compartment—except for a young man who was reading a newspaper. The minister struck up a conversation with the young man and was pleased to learn that he was also a Christian. But he was struggling in his life, often tempted to turn away from his faith. In fact, he was so discouraged that he felt like quitting.

The minister took from his pocket a Bible and a small penknife. "Just watch. I'm going to make this penknife stand up on the cover of this Bible in spite of the rocking of the train."

The young man, thinking this was some kind of trick, watched with interest. "I'm afraid that won't be very easy to do, sir."

"But," said the minister, "I'm doing it."

"But you are holding it," retorted the young man.

"Why, of course! Did you ever hear of a penknife standing up on its end without being held up?"

"I see," the young man responded. "You mean that I cannot stand unless Christ holds me. Thank you for reminding me. I was almost ready to give up."

Jude describes Jesus as the One "who is able to keep you from falling and to present you before his glorious presence without fault and with great joy" (Jude 24).

Sometimes my prayer is one the psalmist often prayed: "Please, God, rescue me! Come quickly, LORD, and help me" (Psalm 70:1 NLT), with emphasis on the word *quickly*.

What a comfort to hear Jesus say, "Are not two sparrows sold for a penny? Yet not one of them will fall to the ground apart from the will of your Father. . . . So don't be afraid; you are worth more than many sparrows" (Matthew 10:29, 31).

God sees, God cares, and God will keep you from falling if you will reach out and grasp His strong hand. That's good news. It doesn't all depend on you.

TAKE A BREATH

When you feel you can't keep going a minute longer, know that God's strong arms are there to hold you. When the bills are piled high, the children are sick, your husband has lost his job, and, to top it all off, you've just gained eight unwanted pounds, lift your eyes from your insurmountable problems and look at these promises:

Though he stumble, he will not fall, for the LORD upholds him with his hand. (Psalm 37:24)

Cast your cares on the LORD and he will sustain you; he will never let the righteous fall. (Psalm 55:22)

I was pushed back and about to fall, but the LORD helped me. (Psalm 118:13)

No matter how wobbly you are in your own strength, these promises will hold you up.

I can't stand up any longer, Lord,
not in my own strength.
That's why I'm leaning on You.

Hospitality—
Mary or Martha Style?

Are you a "Mary" or a "Martha"?

As Jesus and the disciples continued on their way to Jerusalem, they came to a village where a woman named Martha welcomed them into her home. Her sister, Mary, sat at the Lord's feet, listening to what he taught. But Martha was worrying over the big dinner she was preparing. She came to Jesus and said, "Lord, doesn't it seem unfair to you that my sister just sits here while I do all the work? Tell her to come and help me."

But the Lord said to her, "My dear Martha, you are so upset over all these details! There is really only one thing worth being concerned about. Mary has discovered it—and I won't take it away from her" (Luke 10:38–42 NLT).

Martha was the one who invited Christ to their home— a generous, loving act of hospitality. Yet serving Christ, which should have been a joy, became a "distraction." She resented Mary for not helping her, probably because Martha had planned too elaborate a meal, beyond what she could handle herself as a gift of love for Christ.

Oh, how I can identify with that! I've so often done the same thing myself. I've invited guests—and then I've hollered at the kids to clean up their rooms, help me set the table, hurry up and change into clean clothes—and, of course, after it's all over, help clean up the mess. No wonder they sometimes didn't enjoy having guests!

Martha was "worried and upset" about many things. What she needed was what Mary had chosen: to spend time at Jesus' feet hearing His Word.

TAKE A BREATH

Lessons to remember:

- The next time you invite someone into your home for a meal, don't attempt anything more elaborate than you can handle. Try not to create a burden that you'll expect the rest of the family to help carry—and then feel resentful if they don't.

- Perhaps guests would rather be listened to than served a gourmet meal.

- Service for the Lord should be a sacrificial love gift

to Him with no thought of whether or not others are also sacrificing.

• The cure for being distracted, worried, and upset is time at Jesus' feet, listening to His Word. That will require adjusting your priorities.

• When the Lord wants to talk to you, your service for Him is no substitute for your undivided attention.

Lord, gently remind me the next time
I have guests to keep my eyes on You.

Time to Think

When our kids were small, I struggled with finding time to read my Bible and pray. It seemed to me that life wasn't fair—I wanted to have a close relationship with the Lord, yet the bathroom was the only place where I ever had a minute to myself. (How many moms have locked themselves in that smallest room in the house just to have a few moments to think!) Often the best I could do was grab a couple verses on the run and send S.O.S. prayers to God.

A well-known Christian author wrote, "We are too busy only because we want to be too busy." What do you think about that statement? Is it true?

Let's say you're a single mom. You rarely have any time for yourself. You have a tremendously heavy load of responsibilities—caring for your kids, earning a living, running all the errands, even fixing leaky faucets—and that's just what you do when everyone stays well and life is relatively normal. When even one of the kids is sick, your load is still heavier. Are you too busy only because you want to be? I hardly think so!

People are busy for different reasons. Some of us want

to accomplish certain tasks, and we're willing to live under tremendous pressure in order to finish them. Others choose to be busy because they find they get the most done when they're under the pressure of time. Who of us hasn't straightened up the house in ten minutes when learning that guests were on their way for a visit! Some find they're happiest when they're very busy—they thrive on activity. Many others stay busy, sadly, as a form of escape so they won't have to think about life.

Are you too busy? You probably are. Then wouldn't it make sense to take a few hours of your life to set priorities for the *rest* of your life? It won't be easy. In *The Sacred Romance,* the author says, "If I try to hold still, my soul reacts like a feather in the afternoon breeze, flitting from place to place without purpose or direction. . . . I become aware that my very identity is synonymous with activity."[19]

Jesus recognized that we need times of rest and quietness. At one point when life was extremely hectic, Mark recorded, "Then, because so many people were coming and going that they did not even have a chance to eat, he said to them, 'Come with me by yourselves to a quiet place and get some rest'" (Mark 6:31).

Time to be quiet and think will seldom happen unless you plan for it. But it's a choice that can change your life.

TAKE A BREATH

Finding time to gather your thoughts is worth your effort.
Here are a few ideas how you could structure that time:

1. Start out with prayer—not using words but just speechless silence in the awesome presence of God. Finish this time by earnestly asking for His guidance.

2. Then jot down on paper a few sentences describing where you are in life. Getting your education? Pursuing a career? Planning marriage? Raising a family? Caring for elderly parents? Coping with serious health problems? Write how you feel about this stage of life. In your Bible look up the following scriptures, and next to them write how they apply to your life:

   - Psalm 31:15

   - Jeremiah 29:11

   - Isaiah 58:11

   - John 8:12

3. Next write down what you think God's priorities are for this period of your life. Be realistic. God

never asks you to do the impossible, but be willing to make changes.

4. Put yourself in God's hands—literally abandon yourself to Him, and in prayer ask His help as you pursue His priorities for you.

Remind me, dear Jesus, to make time for quiet moments.

When You Need Rest

A lady in her eighties took her very first plane ride. Naturally, she was a bit nervous, but she made the trip just fine. When the plane landed, a newspaper reporter was on hand to ask her, "So how was it?"

"Wonderful!" she replied. "But, of course, I never did let my full weight down."

That's me, that's me! So often I'm tense and uptight. I'm making the trip okay, but I'm not letting my weight down—on the Lord. I'm working as if it all depended on me, but I'm forgetting that I'm to rest as if it all depended on Him—which it really does.

Jesus said, "Come to me, all you who are weary and burdened, and I will give you rest" (Matthew 11:28). He doesn't tell us to pretend we're not carrying a heavy load; most of us truly are weighed down with a great many responsibilities. But He invites us to come to Him with our burdens and find His rest. In His presence, we learn that we can have peace in the middle of problems when we learn we can depend on Him. God will not give us more than we can bear. He will engineer the circumstances of our lives in such a way that ultimately He is glorified and we are blessed—if we truly rest in Him and not insist on our own way. As Oswald Chambers said, "Let God engineer."

But often we don't lean on the Lord as fully as we could. See if you don't agree that the following is one of the saddest verses in the Bible:

> This is what the Sovereign LORD, the Holy One of Israel, says: "In repentance and rest is your salvation, in quietness and trust is your strength, but you would have none of it. (Isaiah 30:15)

Here is the great Creator of heaven and earth offering human beings His rest. He sees humanity struggling with burdens far too heavy for them to carry. But they choose to slog away in their own strength rather than turning to the One who offers to help.

The God of eternity knows that we need repentance and rest to be saved, trusting what He accomplished at Calvary, not our own efforts. And we need quietness and trust to have strength for the journey as well. How sad to turn away from this One who is all we need!

TAKE A BREATH

If you are "weary and burdened" today, come to the Lord. "Give all your worries and cares to God, for he cares about what happens to you" (1 Peter 5:7 NLT). Do it right now. Lay your load on the Lord and rest in Him.

Remember, you are not an orphan! You are God's child. Never forget it.

Okay, Lord, I'm letting myself drop into Your hands.
I'm tired of carrying my heavy burdens. I'm exhausted from
keeping up with my life's demands. So I'm going to
just lay myself down on Your promises and rest.

FOR ISSUES
OF THE
HEART

Inspiration for

Real-Life Concerns

POSSESSIONS

A well-dressed man was driving a beautiful BMW convertible in the lane next to mine. On the back of his car was a sticker that said in bold lettering:

Don't let the car fool you
My treasure is in Heaven

The slogan made me smile. Here is a man who obviously enjoys what he owns but doesn't let it own him. That's exactly what Paul told us to do:

Now let me say this, dear brothers and sisters:
The time that remains is very short. . . . Those in
frequent contact with the things of the world should
make good use of them without becoming attached
to them, for this world and all it contains will pass
away. (1 Corinthians 7:29, 31 NLT)

Someone e-mailed me an excellent piece called "The Fate of Sand Castles." No author was given, so I can't give proper credit for the thoughts. But they're too good not to pass on.

There are some children on a beach. They're playing and giggling—building sand castles all the while. They seem so intent on the project. You get amused at how meticulous and careful they are with crumbly corners and towers.

Then a big wave begins building and starts toward shore. But the kids don't panic. Instead, they do the strangest thing. They jump to their feet, scream with delight, and watch the torrent of water wash away their creations. There is no panic. No bitterness. Even children know the inevitable end of sand castles. They are neither surprised nor angry about what has happened.

You and I should be so wise. The stuff of this world is about as lasting and durable as children's sand castles on the beach. Yet we grown-ups can get caught up in it, defensive of it, and depressed over the loss of it.

Children know that their sand castles are brief joys destined to disappear with an incoming tide. So they don't fret as the waves approach. They watch their creations get swept away without shedding tears. Everything about this life is fleeting and perishable. Like sand castles, nothing done for the sake of this world can last. Only what we do for eternity will survive.

Life is God's gift. Revel in every good thing. But as you enjoy your creations in the sand, just remember not to get overly attached to them.

Yes, we must keep a loose hold on material things. Paul said this attitude is for our own good: "I am saying this for your benefit, not to place restrictions on you. I want you to do whatever will help you serve the Lord best, with as few distractions as possible" (1 Corinthians 7:35 NLT).

Think about it.

TAKE A BREATH

Imagine a great wave is sweeping toward your life. What achievements and possessions would you want to save from destruction? You might want to jot down a list.

It's not wrong to take pride in your accomplishments, nor is it a sin to enjoy the physical things God has given you. But if you find yourself spending energy defending them against the advance of time, worrying and fretting over the possibility of their loss, then maybe it's time to ask God to help you loose your hold on this earth. One by one, offer up the items on your list. Give them as love offerings to God. Only then will you be truly free, the way small children are free to delight in life's pleasure.

Thank You, for all You've given me, God.
Remind me to always focus on the Giver rather than the gifts.

FEAR OF DEATH

The man lived in China, and his story is a true one. He had been an idol-maker by trade. But when it came time to die, his idols brought him no peace. Instead, he sensed evil spirits all around him. Terror filled his heart—as though Satan himself were holding him in his clutches. In desperation, he asked his family to pray that the evil spirits would go away, but he got no relief.

Finally, a Christian came to his home and told him he needed to repent of his sins and put his faith in Jesus Christ as his Savior. Would he do it? Oh, yes, he said—anything to get rid of the terror that was haunting him. He bowed his head and asked the Lord to forgive him and come into his heart. Immediately the terrible fear left. The dreadful anxiety that had so tormented him was replaced by the peace of God.

When I heard this story, I immediately thought of Hebrews 2:14–15:

> [Jesus]. . .shared in their humanity so that by his death he might destroy him who holds the power of death—that is, the devil—and free those who all their lives were held in slavery by their fear of death.

Held in slavery! What a fitting way to describe people who are terrorized by the thought of death! I've met women who had to medicate their fears before they could get on a plane to fly. Traveling by boat was no improvement. Perhaps you are like this. My heart goes out to you. Like a slave, you are shackled by fear.

We all try to stay out of harm's way—it's our natural sense of self-preservation. Mark Twain once said that he wished he knew where he was going to die, because if he did, he'd never go near the place!

Yet we do not have to be haunted by the fear of dying, for Christ came to set us free from its slavery. Paul wrote, "Our Savior, Christ Jesus. . .has destroyed death and has brought life and immortality to light through the gospel" (2 Timothy 1:10).

Furthermore, Paul says that when Christ came into your life, "You did not receive a spirit that makes you a slave again to fear, but you received the Spirit of sonship. And by him we cry, 'Abba, Father'" (Romans 8:15).

Instead of a cruel master holding death over our heads, we have a kind Father who says, "Don't be afraid. You are My daughter. I will watch over you. And at the end of this life, I will take you to be with Me forever. You don't have to be afraid."

My friend Donna Pearson, an emergency room nurse, has been at the bedside of many dying people. I asked her if she saw any difference between how believers in Jesus Christ faced death and how those who were not believers faced the same circumstance. She said, "I've seen panic in the eyes of dying people who don't know the Lord. Even their breathing is different as they make every effort to claw their way back to life, bargaining and making deals with God."

In stark contrast, Donna can never forget a certain small elderly man who was brought into the emergency room with cardiac arrhythmia. While he was there, his heart stopped, and he lapsed into unconsciousness. The doctor immediately defibrillated his heart and literally brought him back to life. "Don't do that again!" the gentleman said sharply. "I was with Jesus, and you brought me back. Now, don't do that again!"

What a difference!

TAKE A BREATH

Jesus conquered death and came back to tell us about it. That's why we don't have to be afraid. Think of death as a doorway to His presence in heaven. He's on the other side of that door to welcome us as His children to more freedom, more joy, more satisfaction than anything you could possibly imagine in this life.

Lord, thank you that I don't have to fear death.
Remind me that You will never allow me to be
separated from Your love—so why should I fear?

WORRY

Someone said that worry is misuse of the imagination—and when it comes to worry, most of us have a *great* imagination. "What if. . ." thoughts come to us at all hours of the day and night. "What if my son doesn't get good enough grades to get into college?" "What if the doctor's report says I have cancer?" "What if _____" —you can fill in the blank with your own latest worry.

It seems to be our nature as women to mull over things in our minds. When I've been to a party, I come home, crawl in bed—and then before I fall asleep, my mind goes over and over the events of the evening, remembering who was there, what we talked about, and—let's be honest—what they wore! Scripture says that after the shepherds came to Bethlehem to see the baby Jesus, Mary, His mother, "treasured up all these things and pondered them in her heart" (Luke 2:19). I think this "mulling tendency" is part of our nature.

Perhaps it follows, then, that women are better worriers than men are.

"Don't worry about anything; instead, pray about everything," scripture tells us (Philippians 4:6 NLT). Prayer, then, is the antidote to worry. In my experience, however, just praying once about something does little to keep me from worrying. Every single time that worry comes back to my mind, I find I need to pray about it again. In fact, it works best for me if I do my worrying as part of my prayer, bringing God into the conversation and pouring out my heart's concern to Him. The only way worry goes away is if I pray about the worry until God puts peace in my heart. Maybe sometimes we give up praying too soon.

My favorite verses in the Bible about worry are those well-known ones in Matthew 6:25–34 where Jesus talks about the Father's care for the birds and the lilies. An anonymous poet summed them up well:

> When the birds begin to worry, and the lilies toil
>   and spin,
> And God's creatures all are anxious, then I also may
>   begin;
> For my Father sets their table, decks them out in
>   garments fine,
> And if He supplies their living, will He not provide
>   for mine?

The assurance that He will provide for all my needs brings peace to my worrying mind.

TAKE A BREATH

Rick Warren says, "If you can worry, you can meditate, for worry is negative meditation." It's the focus of our thoughts that makes the difference between meditation and worry. When we focus our thoughts on God and His promises, our outlook changes. Life gets back into perspective. We will still think about the issues in our lives, but we bring God into the picture, and that makes all the difference in the world.

Teach me, Lord, to turn my worrying into prayer.

GREED = IDOLATRY?

We're told to "put to death" some pretty nasty sins in Colossians 3:5—sexual immorality, impurity, lust, evil desires, and greed. It's that last one that caught my attention—greed. Paul says it's really idolatry.

How could greed be idolatry? I mean, when I see things in the mall that I'd like to have—a beautiful lamp, an expensive pair of shoes, some exquisite piece of jewelry (the real kind, you know)—I admit that my craving is sometimes greed. After all, I already have all the basics I need—and many of the luxuries. But is that idolatry? Well, if I want something more than I want God, then my desire is greed—and that is really idolatry.

I'm reminded of Eve, who saw the forbidden fruit, wanted some, took it, and ate it. Such a small thing, that fruit—who would have thought it would really matter all that much? But she definitely wanted that fruit more than she wanted God. In economics, the buyer is called a "consumer." But sometimes our desire for "things" consumes *us*. We want something so badly that it's all we can think of.

So, is my desire always greed? Not necessarily. But I'd better check before I let that craving "consume" me.

When it comes to materialism, it's possible we can go to the other extreme, thinking, "God would never want me to buy anything nice, because it's a waste of money." That kind of thinking often rises from a low sense of our worth in God's sight and, I think, is a discredit to God. Paul instructed, "Command those who are rich in this present world not to be arrogant nor to put their hope in wealth, which is so uncertain, but to put their hope in God, who richly provides us with everything for our enjoyment" (1 Timothy 6:17). Clearly, God intends for us to enjoy the things He gives us.

But it would be a shame to let anything become an idol in my life so that I want it more than I want God.

TAKE A BREATH

How can you distinguish between normal healthy desires and the greed that equals idolatry? The test is in Colossians 3:17: "And whatever you do, whether in word or deed, do it all in the name of the Lord Jesus." When I see that item in the mall, the questions to ask myself go beyond the familiar "Do I need it, can I afford it, and do I have a place to put it?" How about this question: "Can I buy it 'for Jesus' sake'?" Or does He have a better use for this money?

Lord, let me desire nothing so much as Your presence in my life.

ALL THOSE
ANNOYING INTERRUPTIONS

You have a lot of things you want to accomplish today, right? You get up a little earlier than usual to get started. So far so good. But then the telephone rings. It's not a quick call. No, it's someone who needs to talk—and talk—and talk. Eventually, the conversation is over. You hang up and go back to your work. But only until your son calls, saying he forgot his school project that is due at noon today—and can you please bring it to him? Oh, well, it's only the morning. Surely this afternoon you'll get back to your work. But shortly after lunch, your neighbor knocks at your door. She has had an emergency come up. Could you please help? Of course, you tell her. And there goes your day.

Do you hate being interrupted? I have to admit that I do. That's why I'm encouraged by what Annie Keary wrote:

> I think I find most help in trying to look on all interruptions and hindrances to work that one has planned out for oneself as discipline, trials sent by God to help one against getting selfish over one's

work. Then one can feel that perhaps one's true work—one's work for God—consists in doing some trifling haphazard thing that has been thrown into one's day. It is not a waste of time, as one is tempted to think. It is the most important part of the work of the day—the part one can best offer to God. After such a hindrance, do not rush after the planned work; trust that the time to finish it will be given sometime, and keep a quiet heart about it.[20]

After the dust settled from the attack on New York City's Twin Towers, stories began to surface of why some people were alive and others died in the tragedy. Most of those stories were just about the little things that happen to all of us.

- The head of the company got in late that day because his son started kindergarten.

- Another fellow was alive because it was his turn to bring donuts for his fellow workers.

- Then there was the man who put on a new pair of shoes that morning and started off to work. But before he got there, he developed a blister on his foot. He stopped at a pharmacy to buy a Band-Aid. That is why he is alive.

Someone wrote to me in an e-mail: "Now when I am stuck in traffic, miss an elevator, turn back to answer a ringing telephone. . .all the little things that annoy me. . .I think to myself, this is exactly where God wants me to be at this very moment. Don't get mad or frustrated; praise God instead because God is at work watching over you."

Psalm 31:15 says, "My times are in your hands"—God's hands. Truly, peace comes when we decide to let God's hands control our life—instead of the hands of the clock.

May God continue to bless you with all those annoying things.

TAKE A BREATH

Whenever life interrupts your plans—whether it's an unexpected caller, a long line at the grocery store, a traffic jam on your way home from work, or a sick child on the day you had hoped to finish a project—make a practice of saying this prayer: "Lord, my times are in Your hands."

Don't let me be ruled by my schedule.
Keep me flexible enough to hear Your voice
whispering through my life's interruptions.

REVENGE

Since I'm made in God's image, I can, to some extent, discern good and evil. So when I see a terrible wrong done, I want to settle the score on the spot and make the wrongdoer suffer. But God says that's not my job—it's His.

> Never pay back evil for evil to anyone. . . . Dear friends, never avenge yourselves. Leave that to God. (Romans 12:17, 19 NLT)

That makes me feel somewhat let down. When I'm really angry about an injustice, and I read in the Bible that revenge is not my job but God's, it's as if someone put a pinhole in the balloon of my "righteous" anger and the air is slowly leaking out. I *want* revenge. I would have taken a great deal of pleasure going after the person who did wrong. It's not fair that the person gets away with wrongdoing!

But wait just a minute. There's more to that scripture. "For it is written, 'I will take vengeance; I will repay those who deserve it,' says the Lord" (verse 19).

Now, that I like! Right or wrong, it brings me great pleasure to know that in the end, God will punish wrongdoing. They won't get away with it! The evil person who kidnaps children and molests them will one day feel God's vengeance for the evil deeds. The man who leaves his wife and six children to fend for themselves while he shacks up with a girl half his age will not go free. The executive who fleeces her company of vast sums of money that doesn't belong to her, leaving retired investors in dire financial straits, will one day answer to God for the crime.

Yeah, God! Go get 'em!

In researching the subject of revenge, however, I came across another verse that tells me what my responsibility is when I want revenge. "Never seek revenge or bear a grudge against anyone, but love your neighbor as yourself. I am the LORD" (Leviticus 19:18 NLT).

Yes, but what about the police? Does that mean that they should just look the other way when a crime is committed? No, of course not. Scripture teaches that government is God's authority to punish those who do wrong (see Romans 13:1–3; 1 Peter 2:13–14).

Individually, however, I am not to try to settle the score. I am to forgive and seek to love that person, as hard as that may be. The Bible also tells me to pray for my enemies.

Actually, it's the exact opposite of getting revenge.

So when wrong is done and I want revenge, I'm not to settle the score myself, nor should I "stuff" the rage inside. I'm to turn those feelings over to God and simply let Him deal with the wrongdoer in His own way. In the meantime,

I'll have my hands full with my part, which is forgiveness, love, and prayer.

Okay, God. Vengeance is yours. Besides, You'll do a better job than I could ever do.

TAKE A BREATH

The next time you want to take vengeance against someone, remember what Jesus said to those who were accusing the woman caught in adultery: "If any one of you is without sin, let him be the first to throw a stone at her" (John 8:7). We are all guilty of something. What if it were up to others to judge our sin?

When I'm tempted to throw stones, Jesus,
remind me that I live in a glass house.

The Warfare
in My Head

Have you ever tried to stop thinking—to empty your mind of any thoughts whatsoever? Try it! Very quickly you'll realize the best you can do is to think that you are not thinking! God has created us in such a way that we *never* stop thinking.

I find that a lot of the battles of life take place in my mind. Especially in the middle of the night, I find myself struggling to find solutions to nagging problems. Worry shoots holes in my rest. Painful memories from the past pop up to destroy the peace of God that should rule my life. Issues that I thought were settled long ago rear their ugly heads. Fortunately, the apostle Paul tells me how to deal with this: "We take captive every thought to make it obedient to Christ" (2 Corinthians 10:5).

When he tells us to "take every thought captive," Paul is using warfare terminology. In combat, when a soldier is captured as a prisoner, his weapon is taken away and he is confined. No longer is he a threat. Since he is now powerless, he must do pretty much what his captors tell him to do.

Although we can't stop thinking, we can control what thoughts occupy our minds. And it's that battle to control our thoughts that is the first line of attack in our spiritual life.

Thoughts can be "bratty kids" that sap your strength and make your life miserable. Maybe you are filled with jealousy of another woman's beauty. Perhaps daydreaming makes you wish you were in someone else's arms at night. Or you may be filled with hateful thoughts toward your father who molested you. Worst of all, your thoughts may be of self-destructing suicide.

But you are not helpless against these devastating thoughts. You can control what your mind dwells on. You can hold your thoughts accountable to the certainties of God's Word.

Martin Luther said, "You can't keep the birds from flying over your head, but you can keep them from making a nest in your hair." When a thought comes that conflicts with what you know to be true about God, you need to take it "captive"—disarm it by replacing it with a truth from God's Word. That way we make our thoughts "obedient" instead of letting them run wild.

Jesus did exactly that when the devil tempted Him in the wilderness. Some of those temptations were very attractive—to turn stones into bread when He had not eaten in forty days, to bypass the cross and become ruler of the kingdoms of this world, and to show off His miraculous power so that everyone would gasp and say, "Wow!" But

Jesus wasted no time in meeting each thought with a quotation from the scriptures (see Matthew 4). By walking in His steps and following His example, we, too, can take hostage the destructive thoughts that would defeat us.

TAKE A BREATH

It's true that I can never stop thinking. But it makes a world of difference when I cling to what I know to be true about God and insist that my thoughts fall in line. Focusing on God's Word helps me win the warfare in my head.

On the battleground of my mind, Lord,
help me to take my thoughts captive
so that the Enemy's power will be destroyed.

WHEN YOU WANT TO MAKE A DIFFERENCE

Inspiration to
Influence the Lives of Others

STRENGTHENING
OTHERS IN GOD

David was in grave danger. He had been anointed to be the future king of Israel. But Saul, who was the reigning king, was still very much alive and on the throne. Understanding the threat that David was to his rule, Saul wanted nothing more than to have David dead.

Ironically, Saul's son Jonathan was an extremely close friend of David's. Even though Saul wanted David out of the picture, Jonathan maintained his friendship with David at great risk, which, I'm sure, did not make him very popular with his father. The king's son was an enormous encouragement to David.

Jonathan did not, however, merely strengthen David with friendship. He pointed David to God as his source of strength. Notice these words in 1 Samuel 23:16: "Saul's son Jonathan went to David at Horesh and helped him find strength in God." I don't know how Jonathan did it, for the Bible doesn't tell us. But he was a great support to David and a spiritual strength as well.

The day came when Jonathan was no longer there to encourage David in the Lord. The anointed king-to-be was on his own. But David had learned from Jonathan how to find God's strength, for when his friend wasn't there, David strengthened *himself* in the Lord. The Bible tells us that. "David was greatly distressed because the men were talking of stoning him. . . . But David found strength in the LORD his God" (1 Samuel 30:6). Jonathan had taught by example, and David benefited.

Perhaps God wants you to be a Jonathan to a friend who is going through a difficult time. The last time you were in need, God may have made a certain scripture verse come alive to you, and now you could share that verse with your friend. Send him an e-mail, give her a call, drop them a note, or mail a card. Don't preach to her—just give her confidence that God is going to see her through this hard period of time.

TAKE A BREATH

Has anyone ever spoken a word of support to you? Has anyone ever urged you to hang in there and trust God when you felt like giving up? Now it's your turn to reach out and make a difference.

Never underestimate the difference you can make at this moment in your friend's life. Let God use you to be an encouragement. Be the signpost that points her to the Lord. Maybe today is the day that you, like Jonathan, can help your friend find strength in God.

Thank You, Lord, for the "Jonathans" in my life.
May I in turn point my friends toward You.

Finish the Job

I still have the report card. In the comments section, my second-grade teacher wrote, "Darlene has trouble finishing what she starts." Oh, she put it nicely, adding that I tended to put so much detail into my work that I ran out of time to complete it. I think it was just a nice way of saying that, as the saying goes, I tended to bite off more than I could chew.

She was right. I've fought this tendency all my life. Time management is not one of my strong points. You can ask my husband.

Halfway through writing *Encouraging Words for Women*, I noticed a certain verse in the Bible—well, to put it more accurately, the verse stood out as if it were written in neon lights:

Now finish the work, so that your eager willingness
to do it may be matched by your completion of it.
(2 Corinthians 8:11)

"Thank you, Lord," I prayed. "I need that." And I still do as the editor waits for the last four selections for this book.

Finish the job, Paul says in 2 Corinthians. The context of this verse is that the church in Corinth had been the first to come up with the idea of making a financial gift to needy Christians—and, Paul says, they were the first to actually put their idea into action. They deserved a pat on the back for their willingness to reach out to help their hurting Christian brothers and sisters. But apparently the commitment was never completed. Maybe in their enthusiasm they promised a certain amount but had given only part of the money. At any rate, Paul now encourages them to "finish the job."

Paul was a good example for them to follow, for he put into practice exactly what he preached. Near the end of his life, he could say, "I have finished the race" (2 Timothy 4:7 NLT).

Many a half-knit baby afghan sits somewhere in a drawer amid skeins of yarn waiting for its creator to complete it. (The baby it was intended for is now in school!) A Bible study book lies unfinished on a shelf under a stack of half-read books. It's so easy in the enthusiasm of the moment to start something—a new hobby, a new project, or a new ministry. But it's how we finish that matters.

Having written that, I will get on with finishing up this book.

TAKE A BREATH

Not every job is worth finishing. Sometimes, partway into a project, we discover that it's not worthwhile doing after all.

There's no point in finishing. In fact, it would be a waste of time and energy. But when God has spoken to your heart about something He wants you to do, the best possible thing you can do is to finish the job. Even Jesus said, "My nourishment comes from doing the will of God, who sent me, and from finishing his work" (John 4:34 NLT).

Lord, give me the strength to finish the work
You've called me to do.

The Difference
Words Make

In her book *Truffles from Heaven,* Kali Schnieders tells of the difference that encouragement made in her life. Because of Kali's extreme shyness, her mother enrolled her in a speech class. There is nothing more terrifying for a timid person than to have to get up in front of people and talk! After trembling her way through the speech, Kali dashed from the room to read the teacher's evaluation in private.

> There at the top of the page in red ink, Mr. Shipp had forcefully written my grade. I was amazed. Three simple lines on a white piece of paper, formed the letter A. Those three small lines were followed by three HUGE words that changed my life: *Good job, Kali.*

That was the beginning of a new direction in Kali's life. She eventually became, of all things, a speaker for church groups and other organizations—all because someone believed in her.[21]

Barnabas, who lived in the days of the early New Testament church, was like Kali's teacher. His real name was Joseph, but the apostles called him Barnabas, which means Son of Encouragement (see Acts 4). Why?

Well, Barnabas took a man named Saul under his wing and believed in him when nobody else did; he introduced Saul to the church leaders, telling them of Saul's miraculous conversion. Saul became the apostle Paul, and the two of them, Paul and Barnabas, traveled and ministered together.

Then, Barnabas took his cousin John Mark under his wing, a rather immature young man who had disappointed Paul to the extent that Paul no longer wanted to travel with him. Barnabas discipled John Mark until one day Paul wrote, "Get Mark and bring him with you, because he is helpful to me in my ministry" (2 Timothy 4:11). No doubt it was Barnabas's caring that encouraged John Mark to make something of his life.

Never underestimate the difference your support can make in a person's life. Maybe someone is just waiting to hear those words, "Good job, friend!"

TAKE A BREATH

Here's a challenge for you. Just for today, why don't you see how many people you can encourage with your words— yes, simply the things you say. Start with your own family and friends. Let your encouraging words spill over to those you work with. Perhaps you'll meet up with people you don't even know whom you can encourage.

Please use me, Lord, to speak words of encouragement to someone today.

THE COST OF
ENCOURAGEMENT

Was the apostle Paul ever afraid? I mean, really scared? How about being disheartened or "down"? Do you think Paul ever experienced depression? Yes, very definitely.

It happened in Macedonia. While he was in Troas, Paul had a vision of a man from Macedonia standing there begging him, "Come over to Macedonia and help us" (Acts 16:9). After Paul had seen the vision, he got ready at once to leave for Macedonia, concluding that God had called him to preach the gospel to them.

I'm sure he expected wide-open doors of opportunity with great results. He probably figured, "If God has gone to this much bother to send us here, He must have a great harvest."

Instead, this is what happened (in his own words): "When we arrived in Macedonia there was no rest for us. Outside there was conflict from every direction, and inside there was fear" (2 Corinthians 7:5 NLT). The next verse also intimates that he was "downcast"—discouraged. He experienced clashes, fears, exhaustion—nothing but hassles at every turn.

Now, if I were in that situation, I might have wondered,

"Did I make a mistake? Was I really supposed to come here? This isn't working out the way I thought it would." But Paul didn't seem to be surprised, for of course he was used to hard times. But just because he wasn't surprised by trouble didn't mean he didn't get scared and disheartened.

How did he get out of the doldrums? By a visit from someone very dear to him—Titus. This man Titus was a Christian leader who traveled much as Paul did, helping the churches, appointing elders in various towns to lead the fellowships, teaching and encouraging the leaders and teachers. Paul called him "my true son in our common faith" (Titus 1:4).

I'm sure many times Paul had encouraged Titus, but it was time now for Titus to encourage his "spiritual father." Notice Paul's words: "But God, who comforts the downcast, comforted us by the coming of Titus." Just when Paul was up to his ears in conflicts and fears and exhaustion, along came Titus to encourage him.

In many places in the letters Paul wrote, we read about such men as Tychicus, Onesimus, and Timothy—people Paul sent to encourage fellow Christians. Travel cost money in those days, just as it does today. You might ask, "Couldn't that money have been better spent spreading the gospel?" But Paul understood the importance of encouragement. "Therefore encourage one another and build each other up, just as in fact you are doing," he wrote to the believers in Thessalonica (1 Thessalonians 5:11).

Is there someone who needs your encouragement by a visit? You may say, "Yes, but that's expensive! I'd have to buy a plane ticket to get there." Yes, sometimes encouragement is costly. But it pays big dividends. Perhaps your friend is ready to give up because he feels all alone. Maybe she needs to know you care. Oh, I know, you could make a phone call or send a card or an e-mail—that would be a lot cheaper. But sometimes it's just not the same as a personal visit—a warm hug, moments spent over a cup of tea, or time on your knees together asking for God's help.

You may not see a vision of someone calling for help. You may only hear the still, small voice of God saying, "Why don't you go see your friend now?" Are you listening?

TAKE A BREATH

Make a list of the important people in your life, the ones on whom you rely and who count on you as well for emotional support. Now think of things you could do for each person to encourage him or her. Something as simple as sending an e-mail or making a phone call may be exactly what you need to do. But don't rule out actions that cost more, whether in financial or emotional terms. Prayerfully consider how God would use you in the lives of these loved ones.

Thank You, Lord, for all the people who have encouraged me over the years. Show me what I can do in return.

SIGNIFICANCE

Do you like to walk through old graveyards and read the headstones? Some might think it's morbid, but I'm fascinated to see how people's lives are summed up in just a few words. Some of the most meaningful markers I ever saw are in a cemetery in Macau—the gravestones of early missionaries whose lives continue to teach lessons about commitment.

Not all epitaphs are serious, however. The following was reportedly found on a tombstone in England:

> *Remember, man, as you walk by,*
> *As you are now, so once was I,*
> *As I am now, so shall you be,*
> *Remember this and follow me.*

To which someone replied by writing on the tombstone:

> *To follow you I'll not consent,*
> *Until I know which way you went.*

Two epitaphs appear in the Bible in stark contrast with each other, and, oddly enough, both men were kings. One king's name was Jehoram. Scripture sums up his life with the sad words, "He passed away, to no one's regret" (2 Chronicles 21:20). What a tragedy for a man born with so much opportunity for doing good to end up such a failure!

The second epitaph is King David's. In contrast to the epitaph of Jehoram, the apostle Paul said: "When David had served God's purpose in his own generation, he fell asleep" (Acts 13:36). Now, that's an epitaph I'd like to have on my tombstone! I, for one, want to accomplish that purpose for which God has allowed me time here on earth. I want to serve God in my generation. Paul wanted the same thing: "If only I may finish the race and complete the task the Lord Jesus has given me" (Acts 20:24).

The story is told in Mark 14 of a woman who anointed Jesus' feet with very expensive perfume. Some of those present harshly criticized the woman for "wasting" such a precious substance when it could have been sold and the money given to the poor.

"Leave her alone," said Jesus. "Why are you bothering her? She has done a beautiful thing to me. The poor you will always have with you, and you can help them any time you want. But you will not always have me. She did what she could. She poured perfume on my body beforehand to prepare for my burial" (Mark 14:6–8).

The phrase "She did what she could" catches my attention. That became her epitaph, for Jesus said, "I tell you the truth, wherever the gospel is preached throughout the world, what she has done will also be told, in memory of her" (verse 9).

I have a friend who is an example for me. She is in her thirties, single, a businesswoman, and a deaconess in her church. I have never met anyone who was more willing to "do what she could" whenever she sees a need. She seems to have a special gift to sense what a person needs and to reach out to meet that need—whether it's good food, time to rest, some financial help, or a special time for fun. She simply "does what she can" to help. She caught my attention one day when she casually remarked, "I just wish there were more I could do for the Lord." I don't think she fully realizes how significant she is to those whose lives she touches.

Down through the centuries and around the world, people have read in the Bible about the woman who poured out her precious perfume on Jesus' feet because she "did what she could." She achieved significance the same way you and I can—by serving God's purpose in our generation and faithfully doing what we can in our sphere of influence.

TAKE A BREATH

At the start of each day, make a habit of asking God what you can do for Him during the hours ahead. At the end of the day, dedicate all your efforts (whether they seem successful or not) to Him.

Help me, loving Lord, to do whatever I can in Your name.

Putting Love into Action

"Love your neighbor as yourself."

Can I really do that? It all depends on my definition of love. If I wait until I have warm, fuzzy feelings about some people before I love them, I'll be waiting a long, long time.

I like the definition of love that my husband came up with: "an unconditional commitment to an imperfect person to meet the needs of that person in such a way that will require sacrifice." That's the way Jesus loves me. And that's the way He wants me to love others.

In 1992, Jane Wiebe's phone rang and a neighbor frantically asked if she would deliver the evening meal to an apartment near a hospital; five severely wounded Bosnian men were housed there so they could receive the medical treatment they needed.

"No problem. Just give me the address," Jane replied.

She was not prepared, however, for what she found when she arrived. The men could not speak English. Neither could she speak Bosnian. Jane explained:

When I walked into that apartment. . .their faces spoke volumes. Their bodies were mangled and destroyed. One had his eyes blown out by a grenade. One had had his arm blown off. One was paralyzed from the waist down from a bullet in his spine. Another had an infection in his entire leg as he had lain in a Bosnian hospital for nine months with no antibiotics or treatment.[22]

Jane added, "Their grotesque physical wounds were not what captured my very soul. It was their eyes and the total lack of hope that you could read in them. They needed to be loved. . . . I could do that."

In the summer of 1997, she went to Bosnia herself for the first time. Getting off the plane, she was greeted with a sign that read, "Welcome to hell." For seventeen days she lived in a bombed-out home with no water, no electricity— just destruction everywhere. "I could not register that humans could do this to another human. I sobbed and sobbed."

Jane, a former schoolteacher who owns her own business and has three college-age children, could have easily said she had no time to help. Instead, she has made nine missions of mercy to Bosnia, taken tons of food, clothing, and medicines, become fluent in Bosnian, put in a water system in a village that had no running water for six years, started a chicken farm, and sat in hundreds of Bosnian homes, listening to horror stories of war, rape, and massacre. She has sat in on surgeries and brought a seventeen-year-old Bosnian boy to live with her family for six months while he received cancer treatment. The list could go on and on.

We're blessed to have someone like Jane in our world, whose life models how to love your neighbor. Seeing a need, she puts love into action. So can we—with God's help.

Read 1 Corinthians 13:4–7. Ask God to reveal to you specific ways you can make real in your everyday life the kind of love described in these verses.

God of love, thank You for loving me.
May my life make Your love real to others.

For additional help, write to Darlene Sala:

In Asia—
c/o Guidelines International Ministries
P.O. Box 4000
Makati City, MM, Philippines

In the United States—
c/o Guidelines International Ministries
Box G
Laguna Hills, CA 92654

Or by e-mail at—
darlene@guidelines.org

ENDNOTES

1. Linda Dillow and Lorraine Pintus, *Gift-Wrapped by God* (Colorado Springs, CO: WaterBrook Press, 2002), 43.

2. Ruth Harms Calkin, *Tell Me Again, Lord, I Forget* (Wheaton, IL: Living Books, Tyndale House Publishers, 1986), 108.

3. Jack W. Hayford, *The Mary Miracle* (Ventura, CA: Regal, 1994), 99.

4. "Take Time to Smell the Roses," a personal case study on mentoring by Julie Garvey, Lake Forest, CA, 2003, 24.

5. Janet Chester Bly, *Hope Lives Here* (Grand Rapids, MI: Discovery House Publishers, 2000), 106.

6. "Take Time to Smell the Roses," Garvey, 24.

7. Warren Walker, *Release from Tension and Strain* (Indianapolis, IN: Cadle Chapel, n.d.), 11.

8. Madame Jeanne Guyon, *Experiencing the Depths of Jesus Christ* (Sargent, GA: Christian Books Publishing House, n.d.), 34, 35.

9. Quoted in Mary W. Tileston, *Daily Strength for Daily Needs* (Uhrichsville, OH: Barbour, 1990), 191.

10. Philip Yancey, *Reaching for the Invisible God* (Grand Rapids, MI: Zondervan, 2000), 90.

11. Written in 1936 by Mary Stevenson.